Cheese,

You massive cunt!

Love ya son.

Brighton
& Hove
On This Day

Brighton
& Hove
On This Day

Dan Tester

Brighton
& Hove
On This Day

Pitch Publishing Ltd
A2 Yeoman Gate
Yeoman Way
Durrington
BN13 3QZ

Email: info@pitchpublishing.co.uk
Web: www.pitchpublishing.co.uk

First published in the UK by Pitch Publishing, 2014

A CIP catalogue record for this book is available from the British Library.

ISBN: 978-1-909626-68-3
Cover design: Brilliant Orange Creative Services
Typesetting: Alan Wares
Editor: Dan Tester www.copymatters.co.uk
Brighton & Hove Crest courtesy of Brighton & Hove City Council
Printed in Great Britain. Production managed by Jellyfish Solutions.

DEDICATION

RPS

ACKNOWLEDGEMENTS

A big thank you to Tim Carder, who helped kick-start this project by sending me his Brighton Encyclopaedia, all 330,000 words of it!

Thanks, too, to Rob, Tim, Roger, Mitch and Benz for being excellent office mates over the years, for putting up with my rants, but always being there with a pep-talk when required.

Thank you to everyone at Pitch Publishing and in particular, Alan Wares, for typesetting and kindly taking some of the photographs featured on the proceeding pages. And, Dean Rockett for the excellent proofing job.

Sincere thanks must go to some close friends who have encouraged me through the process: (in no particular order) Si, Lucy, Gordon, Claire, Dan P, Annie, Charlie, Mo, Peter, Dan B, Hils, Cheese, Anna, Martin, Jay, Fresh, Sunil, Melissa, Tim, Jules, Lucie, Rob, Caro, Katie, Lee, Gav, Katie, George, Joel, Jay, Andy, Carpet, Paul, Peep Show, Danger, Claw, Klunk, Batters, Hayley, Hoop, Tel, Chris, Rod, Terri, Bod, Lisa, Sarah, Cathy, Ted, and Emma. And, my five godsons for keeping me on my toes!

And my final slice of gratitude goes to every Brightonian for making our home such a great place to be.

FOREWORD

I moved to Brighton over 30 years ago and was always drawn by its unique history and heritage.

Obviously, it was the more salacious and hedonistic traditions that first attracted me but as I fell in love with the place I discovered more and more that it has always had an eccentric and colourful population – and was never dull.

I actually did my university thesis on the development of the town; from its roots as a small fishing village called Brighthelmstone, through bathing machines to amusement arcades to the thriving, vibrant and still slightly leftfield destination it is today.

What my life here and studies have always lacked, however, was a compendium of exactly when all of these events took place.

I have often thought: "What unusual occurrence happened on the 31st July (my birthday) in Hove and what year was it?"

Thankfully, I need wonder no more. This vital information will be constantly at my fingertips…

Norman Cook, February 2014 (Portslade, actually)

INTRODUCTION

The official name of Brighton only came into official use in 1810 after at least 44 variations in the preceding eight centuries including Bristelmestune – as used in *Domesday Book* – Bredhemston, Brichelmston, Brighthampstead, Brighthelmsted, Brighthelnisted, Brighthempston, Brithelmeston, and Brogholmestune.

There are also at least 48 settlements in 11 different countries known as 'Brighton'. It's safe to surmise that none hold quite the same affection to so many people as the city of Brighton and Hove on the glorious Sussex coast of England.

A cultural melting pot, the city – it will always be two towns to me – has attracted creative types, adventurous types, tolerant types, studious types and downright odd types for hundreds of years.

Since the Prince Regent decided to build the Royal Pavilion in the 1800s, the place has become synonymous with creativity, music, hedonism, freedom and, most importantly, tolerance.

There are few places on the planet where a six foot six transvestite can walk, happily, down any street without fear of ridicule. It's one of the many aspects of everyday life that makes Brighton and Hove such a wonderful place to live. You can be what you want here – just be nice doing it!

Brighton & Hove On This Day takes a day-to-day look through the towns' history chronicling nefarious, statistical, salacious, humorous, ridiculous, historical and whimsical highlights that help tell the story of the nation's favourite seaside resort.

From Brighton's first market in 1313, the French invasion of 1545 and 7,000 Brightonians feasting at the first unofficial Brighton Festival in 1817, to bear baiting in Bear Road, the deepest hand-dug well in the world in Woodingdean and the infamous trunk murders, discover the weird and wonderful of Brighton and Hove's rich history in the proceeding pages.

I hope you enjoy reading the book as much as I did writing it.

Dan Tester, February 2014

ABOUT THE AUTHOR

Dan Tester has spent the majority of his life in Brighton and Hove and has a great passion for the place. A lifelong Albion fan, he has written two books on his favourite club – in the same format as this – and also penned a tome on men named Michael!

A copywriter by trade, Dan also writes rubbish poetry, DJs – Northern Soul, funk, disco, Motown and hip hop – at nights across town and beyond, and co-hosts the monthly Family Funktunes show on Radio Reverb.

JANUARY

WEDNESDAY 1st JANUARY 1908

Sir Jack Hobbs made his Test debut for England. The Surrey right-hander is widely regarded as cricket's greatest opening batsman and holds world records in first-class cricket for scoring the most runs (61,237 or 61,760 depending on the source) and centuries (197 or 199). He passed away in Hove in 1963, aged 81. A good innings.

WEDNESDAY 2nd JANUARY 2002

The renowned Hanover Band – widely regarded as the finest orchestra playing period instruments in the world – faced a financial crisis. The Hove-based group needed to find £150,000 by the middle of the month to survive. Chief executive of the group, Stephen Neiman, said; "It has taken 22 years to build the orchestra, which has played more than 1,500 concerts spanning three continents. We have made 160 recordings and it would be a tragedy if it were to disband."

SATURDAY 3rd JANUARY 2000

Brighton-born striker Darren Freeman scored the first goal of the new Millennium in English professional football. The 26-year-old netted after just two minutes in Brighton & Hove Albion's 4-2 Third Division home victory over Exeter City at Withdean Stadium in front of 5,746 fans.

MONDAY 4th JANUARY 1999

Shelagh Diplock, from Hove, was recognised in the New Year's Honours and received the OBE for services to women's rights. She became a director of The Fawcett Society, the first women's suffrage organisation, in 1993 and her work helped to achieve wage parity between the sexes and coincided with an increase in the number of women MPs. "It's great that an award has been made for my work with the group as women's rights have always been seen as something slightly off-beam," said the mother of two in *The Argus*.

WEDNESDAY 5th JANUARY 1831

There were no flashing blue lights when the Brighton Fire Establishment was founded. In the early years of the 19th century, individual fire insurance companies employed groups of fire-fighters to attend only blazes on premises insured by that company.

SATURDAY 6th JANUARY 1973

Maria Colwell was killed by her evil stepfather, William Kepple. Born in 1965, the young girl was fostered at an early age and was a happy child. This changed when she returned to live with her biological mother, Pauline, in Whitehawk, who was no longer co-habiting with Maria's father. She had a new partner, Kepple, who had children of his own, who he clearly favoured. Caring neighbours and teachers communicated concerns to various agencies and, even though she appeared to be 'almost a walking skeleton', she was allowed to remain with Kepple and her step-siblings. She was wheeled in a pram to the Royal Sussex County Hospital on this day with severe internal injuries, including brain damage, and died shortly after arrival. The case resulted in a 41-day public inquiry and on November 2nd 1974 a 'Maria Day' rally was held in Trafalgar Square, London. The thousand people in attendance called for reforms in the law. The result was the passing of the 1975 Children Act, and reforms to social services departments.

FRIDAY 6th JANUARY 2012

Brighton & Hove City Council leader Bill Randall cut the ribbon to mark the official opening of the refurbished Brighton Centre. The improvements included a new front, doors, and foyer, plus a re-design of the restaurant. The redevelopment continued with the replacement of over 4,000 seats and the modernisation of interiors and meeting facilities.

MONDAY 7th JANUARY 1946

The UK release date of *Pink String and Sealing Wax*. The film, set in Victorian Brighton, explored the clash between two very different worlds: the privileged household of a respected chemist Edward Sutton, who rules his family with self-righteous cruelty, and the seedy underworld occupied by a pub landlord's wife, Pearl, her brutal, alcoholic husband, Joe, and her lover, minor villain Dan. A tale of murder, unrequited love, intrigue, ambition and deceit. *EastEnders* it ain't.

THURSDAY 7th JANUARY 1960

Earmarked for considerable redevelopment, the permanent Open Market's 42 stalls welcomed shoppers for the first time. Prior to this, the area had been home to an unorganised selection of barrows, mainly owned by ex-servicemen.

THURSDAY 8th JANUARY 1948

The hotly anticipated world premiere of *Brighton Rock,* the original film of Graham Greene's novel, was held at midnight at the Savoy Cinema in East Street, Brighton.

SUNDAY 9th JANUARY 1966

Fire swept through Hove Town Hall, destroying the Great Hall, the council chamber, and the banqueting hall. The magistrates' court room – which was temporarily housed in the new police building in Holland Road – was unusable, civic records were lost, and the clock tower was badly damaged. A passer-by raised the alarm just past 3am and firemen discovered the Great Hall alight. Just a few hours earlier, 500 revellers were dancing the night away. The three-storey building, constructed in 1882, saw flames shooting 150 feet into the dark night sky. Two hundred firemen rescued a family from a top-floor flat while the mayor's secretary ran into the building and saved the mayor's chain.

WEDNESDAY 10th JANUARY 2001

Hundreds attended a funeral service for former Hove mayor Leslie Hamilton. The congregation at All Saints Church in Hove included Brighton and Hove mayor Andy Durr, the city's three MPs and dozens of councillors – and many ordinary people the 82-year-old had helped as a councillor. His son said in *The Argus*; "He was an ordinary man who left school at 14 for economic reasons but he made an extraordinary mark on public life." Hamilton requested that Jerusalem should be played at his funeral and that there should be no tears. The first request was granted.

SATURDAY 11th JANUARY 1851

The first telegraphic message from Brighton to London was sent by the Electric and International Telegraph Company from Brighton Station. Less than a month later, they opened the first telegraph office at the Royal York Hotel and a rival service was also offered by the London, Brighton & South Coast Railway Company with a system which linked their stations. By 1880 there were 11 telegraph offices in Brighton, plus the railway stations, and nearly half a million messages were handled. Other branch offices opened at Western Road, Hove, in June 1885, College Road in August 1888, and Cannon Place in June 1891, replacing the West Pier office.

AN ODE TO BRIGHTON

I've seen a six-foot-four transvestite driving a bus
Her passengers smile, make no fuss,
I've seen cyclists, thousands, with their bits hanging free
Dancing on the pebbles, with Fatboy, no fee.

I've seen marches; no fox hunting, no war, I want to wear a dress
Save the Albion, the whale, our beloved NHS,
I've seen stags, hens, lads, and cads
West Street at closing, and the ubiquity of fads.

I've seen flares swing and skinny jeans chafe
Winklepickers clop and platforms, unsafe,
I've seen glow sticks, white gloves, freaky dancing
The goths, mods, chavs and whatever's in.

I've seen record shops depart, and hairdressers arrive
Nightclubs close, and students skive,
I've seen beer, and house, prices skyrocket
Weekenders invade, leaving happily out of pocket.

I've seen gays and lesbians liberated in the park
Countless walks of shame long after dark,
I've seen our town, not city, a cultural icon
Forever in my heart, I love you Brighton.

SATURDAY 12th JANUARY 1583

A number of spectators died when a stand collapsed during a bear-baiting event at the Paris Gardens, London. The relevance to Brighton and Hove is that The Bear public house, on the corner of Lewes Road and Bear Road, used to host the barbaric blood sport before its UK ban in 1835.

SATURDAY 12th JANUARY 1963

The biggest freeze of the 20th century played havoc with the football fixture list. Director Harold Paris borrowed a tarmacadam melting machine from the Brighton Corporation to help thaw the Goldstone Ground pitch. Crystal Palace were the visitors for what was one of only four games in the country to survive. The pitch was a quagmire and a goal from Peter Donnelly was not enough to prevent a 2-1 defeat.

FRIDAY 13th JANUARY 1871

By 1870, Brighton's population had risen to 90,000. Just before 1860, the town council decided that all of the town's wastewater should be drained into the sea as the current arrangement of filling cesspools and using the back of dwellings wasn't ideal, or particularly kind on the nostrils. Following detailed surveys, work began in 1865 to improve the situation. About 44 miles of sewers were laid ranging from 30cm diameter salt-glazed ware pipes to 2.4m circular brick tunnels. Inhabitants were not content and in 1869 public pressure grew for an intercepting sewer – a main trunk sewer into which others would drain. An Act of Parliament was obtained in 1870 forming a body called the Brighton Intercepting and Outfall Sewers Board. Work began on the new sewer around this time but it stopped in May when the contractors could not cope with the volume of water encountered. Thirteen pumps of 51 centimetres in diameter were then driven by nine engines to pump an estimated 68 million litres every 24 hours. The resulting intercepting sewer is circular, made of brickwork, is 1.5m in diameter and runs from Hove Street to East Street, and 2.1m thereafter, to Portobello at Telscombe – a total of 7.25 miles. As the Brighton and Hove urban area has expanded so has the sewer system; there are now 300 miles of main sewers running beneath the city. Since the early 1960s, tours of the magnificent Victorian masterpiece have been held from May to September.

THURSDAY 14th JANUARY 1999

Brighton was officially unveiled as the coldest place in the entire universe! A sample of gas inside a glass cell in a corner of a physics laboratory at the University of Sussex had been cooled so that its temperature was only a few hundred billionths of a degree above so-called absolute zero, the coldest possible temperature. Very, very cold!

THURSDAY 14th JANUARY 1999

The Argus reported that the distinctive white cliffs of Beachy Head may turn green. Thousands of tonnes of chalk fell 500ft onto the beach over the previous weekend – one of the biggest losses of British coastline in living memory – spilling 200ft out into the sea. Homes in nearby Birling Gap wanted defences to protect them from additional damage but efforts to stop further falls would change the area's famous white cliffs forever. A spokesman for the Environment Agency said; "Beachy Head is white because it erodes and exposes fresh chalk. If defences were put in you would have a similar situation to Dover, where works for the Channel Tunnel meant the cliffs are now going green with vegetation."

WEDNESDAY 15th JANUARY 2003

Dean George helped England beat Scotland 7-2 in the final of the Home Countries Quadrangular badminton tournament at Cardiff. The 15-year-old from Brighton also collected another gold medal, winning the boys' doubles.

SATURDAY 16th JANUARY 1982

Preston from the Ordinary Boys was born in Worthing. Famous for living in Hove and marrying a 'fake' celebrity, the singer's last solo single, in 2009, peaked at 168 in the UK chart. His ex was last seen in a relationship with cagefighter Alex Reid, who was once married to another Brightonian, Katie Price.

MONDAY 17th JANUARY 1859

Situated in a room off the Royal Pavilion kitchen, provided by the Town Council, the Brighton School of Art opened its doors to more than 50 pupils. New premises for Brighton School of Science and Art were purpose-built in Grand Parade in 1877.

SATURDAY 18th JANUARY 1936

Rudyard Kipling died of a perforated duodenal ulcer at Middlesex Hospital. A purveyor of short-stories, poetry and novels, he is remembered for his tales and poems of British soldiers in India, celebrating British imperialism, and children's stories. Kipling received the Nobel Prize for Literature in 1907, declined British Poet Laureateship and on several occasions turned down a knighthood. Revered works include *The Jungle Book*, *Kim* and *Gunga Din*. He lived in Rottingdean from 1897 to 1903 and has a junior school named after him up the road in Woodingdean.

TUESDAY 19th JANUARY 1999

Boy racers turned the Halfords and B&Q car park along Lewes Road into a temporary 'cruise' venue. More than 200 drivers in around 50 cars gathered after the police closed their regular monthly racing spot on Madeira Drive.

FRIDAY 20th JANUARY 1888

The Clock Tower – 'the only permanent memorial that Brighton has of Her Majesty's Jubilee' wrote the *Brighton Gazette* – was unveiled. Its main feature was the 'time ball', designed by Magnus Volks, and controlled by a landline from Greenwich Observatory, which rose hydraulically up the mast and fell on the hour.

SATURDAY 21st JANUARY 1882

Although not validated, Brighton can probably claim to have the oldest continuous public electricity supply in the world. In 1881, Robert Hammond was employed by shopkeepers to light premises along Queen's Road and Western Road. The Hammond Electric Light and Power Company started supplying power from a generator at the Regent Iron Foundry in North Road, now the Royal Mail sorting office.

MONDAY 21st JANUARY 1980

The Athina B beached to the east of the Palace Pier (see 11/12/1979).

SATURDAY 22nd JANUARY 1966

Filmed two years earlier in and around Brighton, *Smokescreen* was shown on East German TV for the first time. The film starts when a blazing car goes over the cliff at Beachy Head. An insurance investigator is sent to the coast to find out more. The driver had recently taken out life insurance and suspicions mount when no body can be found. The wife who would benefit from the policy, the business partner who has financial troubles, and the person who sold the policy and fancies the wife, are all in the frame.

FRIDAY 22nd JANUARY 1999

After three days of labour, Paula Cooper finally gave birth to Harry Ewens at the Royal Sussex County Hospital; thought to be one of the heaviest babies to ever be born in Sussex. Weighing in at 12lb 1oz, the boy's father, Derek, had to rush out to buy some new clothes. The proud parent said; "After he was born the doctors couldn't believe how big he was. The word soon spread round the hospital and Paula had lots of doctors and nurses just coming to get a look at Harry. The doctors have said he is the biggest baby they have ever seen at the hospital. He certainly caused a bit of a stir." Canadian giantess Anna Bates (1846–88), 7ft 5.5 ins., gave birth to a boy weighing 23lb 12oz at her home in Seville, Ohio, USA on January 19th 1879, but he died 11 hours later.

SUNDAY 23rd JANUARY 2000

Robbie Williams made a surprise appearance in a Brighton pantomime performance of *Aladdin*. The 25-year-old stole the show at the Theatre Royal by singing She's The One to the audience of just under 1,000. Half an hour into the play the stage fell into darkness before a single spotlight suddenly revealed the former Take That member. "We are a 951-seater auditorium. Robbie is more used to playing upwards of 50,000 so it was a very personal performance. He got a standing ovation," enthused stage-door manager, Bill Tinsley.

THURSDAY 24th JANUARY 1935

Brighton Town Council passed a resolution that, subject to the approval of the Minister of Transport, the 30mph speed limit should be enforced throughout the whole of the borough. *The Times* explained; "This will mean that the regulations which the Minister proposes to bring into operation in March will be enforced on 10½ miles of roadway which do not come within the 'built up area' definition. Mr T Morris said that last year 16 people were killed and 461 injured in the streets of Brighton... We do not want speed-mad motorists in town, said Mr Morris. We do not want people to come here to fly through the town at 40 miles an hour. Even animals have the right of protection from this class of motorist, who must be taught that if they come to Brighton they have to behave themselves."

MONDAY 24th JANUARY 1938

A single-seater Bristol fighter, one of four on a formation flight from Kenley, crashed into the side of a house on Lyndhurst Corner in Hove. The pilot landed by parachute in Beaconsfield Road, a mile or so away, in Brighton. His only injuries were a few bruises and a cut tongue.

THURSDAY 25th JANUARY 2007

Jazz singer George Melly collapsed on stage at the Old Market in Hove. The 80-year-old had been suffering from health problems including emphysema and lung cancer. Years of exposure to sound systems ...

... affected his hearing and he joked that his deafness often made boring conversations more interesting. He equated his dementia to a quite amusing LSD trip. His last performance was at the famous 100 Club on Oxford Street, London in June of this year and he passed away the following month.

MONDAY 26th JANUARY 1795

A rapid thaw caused a seven-feet-high flood in Pool Valley. The area is the natural drainage point for most of Brighton, where the Wellesbourne river discharged into the sea. Traditionally a place for fishing boat storage, the area was bricked over three years earlier which resulted in numerous water breaches over the years.

SATURDAY 26th JANUARY 1991

Nearly 7,000 Sussex folk wiped their eyes in disbelief as Albion came back from two goals down at Anfield. A penalty by Mike Small and a late John Byrne header earned an FA Cup replay with league champions Liverpool at the Goldstone Ground. The game will forever be remembered for John 'football genius' Crumplin's superb marshalling of England international winger John Barnes. Nearly 21 years later – and against the same opposition manager Kenny Dalglish – Albion could not repeat their courageous performance, going down 6-1 on Merseyside.

TUESDAY 26th JANUARY 1999

Sussex's oldest resident, Ethel Gale, died three months before her 111th birthday. She lived through two world wars and saw two Queens and four Kings on the throne. Ethel loved a brandy at breakfast to see her through the day – and one in the evening to ensure a good night's sleep – and was a popular figure at her rest home.

SATURDAY 27th JANUARY 1968

The Brighton Corporation announced it was to increase the cost of deckchair hire for the 1968 season to 9d. Hove immediately decreed their charge would remain at 6d!

SATURDAY 28th JANUARY 1961

One of the most celebrated games in Albion's history. Reigning champions Burnley were in town for the fourth-round FA Cup tie which attracted a 28,672 gate. The 3-3 draw included one of the greatest goals ever seen at the Goldstone. Right-back Bob McNicol ran from his own half and unleashed a 35-yard rocket. It was his only goal for the club in 99 appearances!

SATURDAY 28th JANUARY 2006

Sensational scenes at The Triangle, Burgess Hill as NBA basketball legend Dennis Rodman arrives in a white limousine for his Brighton Bears debut against Guildford Heat. The 6ft 6ins cross-dressing eccentric is the leading rebound scorer in the NBA and turned out for the Bears after appearing on TV's *Celebrity Big Brother.* As it transpired, BBL regulations allowed only three players who required work permits and the American's appearance cost his new club three points, an undisclosed fine, and the victory: Bears had won 91-88 but the game was awarded to the Heat, 20-0.

SATURDAY 29th JANUARY 1984

The live TV cameras – a rarity in those days – were present for the visit of champions Liverpool in this FA Cup fourth-round tie. Gerry Ryan dinked the ball home in the 57th minute. Just 60 seconds later and a slide-rule pass saw Terry Connor gallop through to finish from just outside the box, the striker leaping to celebrate as the ball left his right foot. It was another memorable Albion victory over the red half of Merseyside.

MONDAY 30th JANUARY 1837

Well over a century before the London to Brighton bike ride, another race took place... on foot! *The Times* reported: "On Monday morning [today] Townsend and Berry, the pedestrians, started in a race on foot for Brighton, from the Elephant and Castle. Townsend, who had 20 minutes' law given him, started at five minutes past 8, and Berry at 25 minutes past... where again Townsend took the lead, and entered Brighton in triumph, the winner performing the journey in eight hours and 37 minutes. They were both much distressed, but particularly Berry, who was obliged to ride the last four miles into Brighton. The race was for a bet of 100l.–50l. aside. There were many bets depending on the match. Betting, 5 to 4 upon Townsend, who is several years older than Berry." [all sic]

FRIDAY 31st JANUARY 1997

Quadrophenia (1979) was re-released in the UK. The film, set in 1965, follows the story of Jimmy Cooper (Phil Daniels), a working-class London Mod who listens to African-American soul, Jamaica ...

... ska, and British beat music, takes amphetamines and rides Vespa and Lambretta scooters. The story focuses on Jimmy's – and his friends' – pursuit of women, music, suits and drugs and their run-ins with rivals, the Rockers. A Bank Holiday weekend trip to Brighton provides the excuse for the rivalry to come to a head as they both descend upon the seaside. The Mods meet for breakfast at the Waterfront Cafe at the Peter Pan Playground on Madeira Drive and then hit the town. The exterior for the club scene where the Ace Face impresses on the dancefloor is now the Brighton Sealife Centre. A riot spreads from the seafront into town and just across Old Steine into East Street, where the rioters get hemmed in by the police. Jimmy slopes off for a bit of how's yer father with Steph in the narrow alley by number 11, leading to Little East Street. With his beloved scooter written off, no job, no home and lots of pills, Jimmy catches the train to Brighton from Paddington Station (although no trains run to the south coast from there). The hotel, where he is ultimately disillusioned by the sight of the Ace Face working as a bellboy, is the Grand in King's Road. He steals Ace's scooter and heads out to the cliffs at Beachy Head, where he rides towards the cliff edge. The film ends with the scooter smashing on the rocks below. The stunt co-ordinators underestimated the distance that the scooter would fly through the air and the cameraman, who shot the scene from a helicopter, was almost hit.

FEBRUARY

TUESDAY 1st FEBRUARY 1921

The Chattri was unveiled by the Prince of Wales, 500 feet above sea level on the Downs to the north of Patcham Court Farm. Accessed by bridleway only, the memorial – set in two acres of gardens – honours the Indian soldiers who died at the Royal Pavilion when it was used as a hospital in World War I. During the conflict, over one-and-a-half million Indian army soldiers saw active service alongside British troops and around 12,000 who were wounded on the Western Front were hospitalised at sites around Brighton, including York Place School, the Dome, the Corn Exchange and the Royal Pavilion. The 53 Hindu and Sikh soldiers who died in Brighton were taken to a peaceful resting place on the Downs for cremation, after which their ashes were scattered in the sea, in accordance with their religious rites. Now a listed building, the Chattri was erected by the India Office and was designed in white Sicilian marble by student architect E C Henriques. The octagonal, domed monument with 29-feet high pillars on a stone plinth bears the following inscription: 'To the memory of all the Indian soldiers who gave their lives in the service of their King-Emperor this monument, erected on the site where the Hindus and Sikhs who died in hospital at Brighton passed through the fire, is in grateful admiration and brotherly affection dedicated.'

MONDAY 2nd FEBRUARY 1618

The second town book was revised (see 23/07/1580) by the mutual agreement of fishermen and landsmen. The customs and orders set down in the two books were legally binding and could only be repealed by Parliament. One order remains effective to this day; three church-wardens are still chosen for the Parish of Brighton (St Peter's).

TUESDAY 3rd FEBRUARY 2003

The BBC website revealed that Brighton and Hove 'has most gay couples' in England and Wales. For the first time, the official Census was used to estimate the number of gay couples living together. Staff at the Office for National Statistics used the 2001 count of people and households to find there were 78,522 individuals who said they lived with a person of the same sex, 2,544 – 1.29% of the population – of whom were from Brighton and Hove. Not really much of a surprise!

SUNDAY 3rd FEBRUARY 2008

Brighton-born drummer Steve Ferrone played with Tom Petty's band during the half-time interval of Super Bowl XLII – wearing a Brighton & Hove Albion hat – at the University of Phoenix Stadium, Glendale, ...

UBIQUITOUS SEAGULLS GRACE THE PALACE PIER CLOCK TOWER. © ALAN WARES

... Arizona. The musician has recorded with some of the world's leading artists including The Bee Gees, George Benson, Eric Clapton, Rick James, Whitney Houston, Chaka Khan, and Paul Simon. He has yet to perform with fellow Brightonian musician David Van Day.

TUESDAY 4th FEBRUARY 2003

Six weeks before their near neighbour suffered a similar fate, albeit more devastating, there was a fire on the Palace Pier. It began on the ghost train, spread to the amusements nearby, and burnt a hole through the decking. Seven fire crews attended the scene as flames rose thirty feet into the night sky. Thankfully, no-one was hurt and the pier re-opened the following day.

TUESDAY 5th FEBRUARY 1901

Brighton & Hove Albion legend Tommy Cook was born in Cuckfield, 13 miles north of the twin towns. The greatest goalscorer in the club's history, 123 in 209 starts, the centre forward topped the leading scorer charts in three seasons and led the England attack against Wales in 1925 as a Third Division player. An outstanding cricketer too, Tommy made 20,198 runs for Sussex between 1922 and 1937. Tragically, the great man took his own life in 1950 after failing to fully recover from a plane crash in which he was the only survivor.

WEDNESDAY 6th FEBRUARY 1929

Novelist, newspaper columnist, and television writer Keith Waterhouse was born in Leeds. His credits, many with life-long friend and collaborator Willis Hall, include satires such as *That Was The Week That Was*, *BBC-3* and *The Frost Report* during the 1960s and *Worzel Gummidge*. A resident of Embassy Court for many years, he wrote regularly for the *Daily Mirror* and the *Daily Mail* and fought long crusades against the decline in the standards of modern English; he founded the Association for the Abolition of the Aberrant Apostrophe, whose members attempt to stem incorrect usage such as 'pound's' 'apple's' and 'orange's'.

TUESDAY 7th FEBRUARY 2006

The BBC suggested that 9,000 stag and hen weekends descended on Brighton the previous year and they predicted a rise up to 15,000 for 2006. "There are more nightclubs per square mile in Brighton than anywhere else in the UK." There were before the licensing laws changed and the smoking ban came in... Four have disappeared from within a few hundred yards of St Peter's Church alone...

MONDAY 8th FEBRUARY 1960

Edna Best was inducted in the Hollywood Walk of Fame (6124 Hollywood Boulevard). Born in Hove in 1900, the actress – she won a silver swimming cup as the lady swimming champion of Sussex – is best remembered for her role as the mother in the original 1934 film version of Alfred Hitchcock's *The Man Who Knew Too Much*. She also starred in *Intermezzo: A Love Story* (1939), *Swiss Family Robinson* (1940), *The Late George Apley* and *The Ghost and Mrs Muir* (both 1947) and *The Iron Curtain* (1948). She died in Geneva, Switzerland in 1974.

SATURDAY 8th FEBRUARY 1997

A very special day in the history of Brighton & Hove Albion. Fans had been protesting all season and the internet was in its infancy. Plymouth Argyle supporter, Richard Vaughan, suggested on the supporters' forum North Stand Chat that fans from every club in the Football League – and further afield – should lend their support and call for the departure of Bill Archer and David Bellotti by turning up for the Hartlepool United game. Fans United was born. The rain and mist did not dampen the remarkable scenes: fans from clubs around the world roared the Albion to a 5-0 victory. The result effectively saved the club from relegation to the Conference and possible oblivion...

MONDAY 9th FEBRUARY 2009

Around 30 firefighters tackled a blaze at the disused Sussex Ice Rink in Queen's Square, Brighton. Reports suggested squatters were trapped inside the building but this proved to be unfounded. The 60ft by 40ft rink – the only one in the whole county for 30 years after the SS Brighton's demise – closed in May 2003.

THURSDAY 10th FEBRUARY 1881

Electric street-lighting was introduced, as an experiment, when Charles Siemens strung a series of arc-lights along Marine Parade, with a generator installed in an arch below. The streets of Brighton were originally lit by oil lamps until the 1773 Brighton Town Act established the town commissioners for street-lighting. The Pavilion grounds became the first area to be illuminated by gas in September 1818, but the permanent lamp-posts which still stand – now listed structures – were erected in the reign of William IV. In May 1824 the Steine introduced gas lighting and by 1853 there were 947 gas street-lamps in the town.

SATURDAY 11th FEBRUARY 1989

The day before music video director Tim Pope's 33rd birthday, The Bangles released *Eternal Flame* in the UK, which was inspired by two eternal flames, one of which was for Elvis Presley at Graceland. The Brighton resident is responsible for iconic videos including *Happy Birthday* (Altered Images), *Close to Me* and *Friday I'm in Love* (The Cure), *One Way Ticket* (The Darkness), *Everyday I Love You Less and Less* (Kaiser Chiefs), *It's A Hard Life* (Queen), and *It's My Life* (Talk Talk).

THURSDAY 12th FEBRUARY 1579

The Privy Council established a commission of inquiry comprising four local worthies (a worthy or prominent person): Thomas Sackville, one of the lords of the Manor of Brighton and joint Lord Lieutenant of Sussex; the Earl of Arundel, the other lord of the manor; Sir Thomas Shirley of Wiston; and Richard Shelley of Patcham Place. The four petitioned Parliament on behalf of the inhabitants of Brighton – who were principally divided into those dependent on the fisheries, and those supported by crafts and farming (landsmen) – to assist in resolving a dispute between the two parties.

FRIDAY 13th FEBRUARY 1976

Dr Desmond Morris opened the new galleries at the Booth Museum in Dyke Road. Constructed in quite an isolated position in 1874 by Thomas Booth to house his collection of stuffed British birds displayed in their natural habitats, the building now houses one of the country's largest regional natural history collections with 621,000 items, including butterflies, moths, insects, skeletons, reptiles, mammals and geological exhibits.

TUESDAY 14th FEBRUARY 2012

The frequency of commercial flights could increase at Brighton City Airport. Bosses at Shoreham confirmed they are looking to open up the runway to private operators for more chartered services to UK and European destinations.

SUNDAY 14th FEBRUARY 1980

The roads were blocked, the seafront shops were doing a brisk trade and thousands flocked to the beach. There was no heatwave, no Fatboy Slim gig, no protest and no Albion title to celebrate, just the off chance that the stranded *Athina B* would finally set sail again on the expected high tide. An estimated 30,000 spectators lined the front and local bookmakers offered 6/4 against the ship being refloated. A salvage tug succeeded in pulling the huge cargo ship off the shingle and into the sea mist, much to the delight of the cheering crowd. A Salvation Army band played 'Rule Britannia' as a bookie lamented a £2,000 loss by raising a glass of champagne to the departing hunk of metal.

SUNDAY 14th FEBRUARY 2010

The RNLI Brighton Lifeboat was launched as a hot-air balloon ditched into the sea. A member of the public dialled 999 at 7.13pm and described having seen flames ascend from the basket, and ignite the balloon as it landed in the water approximately one mile offshore. Arriving on scene, with excellent visibility, it quickly became apparent to the B and Y boats that it was unlikely to have been a very large balloon as nothing was visible on the surface. Approximately 30 minutes into the search a Chinese lantern was seen drifting overhead and with Chinese New Year celebrations under way at a restaurant near the West Pier, offering an alternative explanation. Sure enough, a few minutes later the lifeboat found the charred remains of a Chinese lantern not far from the position of the reported sighting. A spokesman for Brighton Lifeboat said: "Naturally, our first instinct was that this could have been a major incident and it was approached accordingly with all resources at our disposal. Judging distance and scale while looking seaward at night isn't easy and it's perhaps easy to see how this case of mistaken identity could have occurred."

THURSDAY 15th FEBRUARY 2001

Brighton and Hove officially became a city with the arrival of a document from the Queen. The document, signed by the monarch and known as letters patent – a type of legal instrument in the form of an open letter issued by a monarch or government, granting an office, right, monopoly, title, or status to a person or to some entity such as a corporation – was presented to Brighton & Hove council. The exact wording is: "ELIZABETH the SECOND BY THE GRACE OF GOD OF THE UNITED KINGDOM OF GREAT BRITAIN AND NORTHERN IRELAND & OF OUR REALMS & TERRITORIES QUEEN HEAD OF THE COMMON WEALTH DEFENDER OF THE FAITH. To all to whom these Presents shall come Greeting. Whereas We for divers good causes and considerations Us thereunto moving are graciously pleased to confer on the Towns of Brighton and Hove the status of a city Now Therefore Know Ye that We of Our especial grace and favour and mere motion do by these Presents ordain declare and direct that the TOWNS OF BRIGHTON AND HOVE shall ...

... henceforth have the status of a CITY and shall have all such rank liberties privileges and immunities as are incident to a City. In witness whereof We have caused Our Letters to be made Patent Witness Ourself at Westminster the thirty first day of January in the forty ninth year of our reign. By Warrant under The Queens Sign Manual Phillips." Yes, really.

THURSDAY 16th FEBRUARY 1933

Love Is The Sweetest Thing was number one in the US Billboard chart. It was the first of six 1930s American chart-toppers for the Brightonian bandleader and composer, Ray Noble. He studied at the Royal Academy of Music and became head of the HMV Records studio band in 1929. Noble famously penned the immortal *Goodnight Sweetheart*, in 1931, plus *By The Fireside, I Found You* and *What More Can I Ask*. He passed away, aged 74, in 1978 and was inducted into the Big Band and Jazz Hall of Fame in 1987.

SATURDAY 17th FEBRUARY 1866

The first turf was cut on the Kemp Town branch line by Mayor Henry Martin. The single track – one mile and 726 yards long – left the Lewes line 1,606 yards from Brighton station and was over 2.3 miles long, about twice the distance by road. The three-station-line (Lewes Road, Hartington Road and Kemp Town) – with a viaduct spanning Lewes Road where the Sainsbury's now stands – was closed in 1971 after 39 years as a goods-only route. London Brighton & South Coast Railway – because of rivalries between LB & SCR and London, Chatham & Dover Railway – decided to build the short but expensive branch line, chiefly as a blocking move to prevent another rail route being laid into the town.

WEDNESDAY 17th FEBRUARY 1880

The Times informed the masses about a new event... "The Brighton Festival, under Mr Kuhe's direction, opened last night [today] with great éclat. The dome of the Royal Pavilion was filled to the last seat... The orchestra included some of the ablest London professors, and the chorus of amateurs, although not very large, was efficient... The principal piece of the evening was Mendelssohn's Hymns of Praise, preceded by a new and important sacred cantata, The First Christmas Morn, by Mr Henry Leslie, an able work which deserves more detailed analysis..."

SATURDAY 18th FEBRUARY 1967

First Division Chelsea were the guests for an FA Cup fourth-round tie in Hove. A 35,000 sell-out Goldstone crowd witnessed a 1-1 draw – Dave Turner netted for Albion. The London club's boss Tommy Docherty had this to say in the programme; "They have a First Division set-up at the Goldstone Ground, and First Division ideas, as well as a first-class pitch. The day cannot be far away when they become one of our top clubs."

SUNDAY 19th FEBRUARY 1939

Two days earlier, William Thomas Jones discovered an earthenware pot containing 450 tiny bronze coins while digging a sewage trench on Downland north of Hove. One opinion of the find was that is was from a settlement dating back to AD 50.

SUNDAY 20th FEBRUARY 1983

FA Cup victories for Albion over Newcastle United and Manchester City were rewarded with a fifth-round tie... at Football League champions Liverpool! No team had won at Anfield for almost a year and Albion had been victorious on the road – at St James' Park in the third round – only once all season. Amazingly, Gerry Ryan put the Seagulls ahead just after the half hour. Australian Craig Johnston equalised with an acrobatic strike with 20 minutes remaining only for former Kop favourite Jimmy Case to blast home the winner from 20 yards just 60 seconds later.

WEDNESDAY 21st FEBRUARY 2007

Hove resident Stuart Conway, who had thrown 7,000 bottles into the sea over a ten-year period, was warned by the council that he may be putting bathers in danger. The free online message-in-a-bottle service was set up by the retired data administrator to help romantics. "I like to think of myself as a sort of postman for emotions," he said. "Most people opt for the classic green corked wine bottle. The half bottles of vodka and gin float the best, but magnums are my favourite to throw."

SATURDAY 22nd FEBRUARY 1902

The Albion played their first-ever game at the Goldstone Ground, Newtown Road, Hove, as a Sussex Senior Cup semi-final was taking place at the County Ground, the club's home pitch. The opponents for the historic friendly were Southampton Wanderers, who were thrashed 7-1. The club became the sole occupants in 1904.

MONDAY 23rd FEBRUARY 2009

Margaret Pracy was 'fined' 54p by British Gas for using too little electricity. The Brighton resident used approximately £5 of power a week, which was below the minimum threshold of £9. She had made home improvements under the government's Warm Front initiative.

SATURDAY 24th FEBRUARY 1951

Councillor Lewis Cohen had grandiose plans for Brighton and Hove. *The Brighton Herald* carried this article: "The Brighton of the future will present a vastly different picture from what it does today... To ensure the town's prosperity it must attract visitors all the year round... To give prosperity... we have to plan it as both a residential and a holiday town. New attractions would include a new open-air swimming pool in the centre of town... improved beach facilities with gaily-coloured deck-chairs and umbrellas and canvas bathing stations, a children's playground... Heavy motor traffic along King's Road would be banned, because 'holidaymakers want sea breezes and not petrol fumes'; the Kemp Town and Madeira Drive area would be re-planned with sun terraces and more flowers... Brighton should capitalise on the growing popularity of conferences, because delegates, their wives and friends would return year after year for a holiday if the town appealed to them..."

MONDAY 24th FEBRUARY 1812

From *The Sussex Weekly Advertiser*: "His Royal Highness having declared the formation of a new Ministry unnecessary, the prospect of a dissolution of Parliament has vanished, to the great disappointment of many, and especially to those friends of freedom." The government was under threat from rival politicians, and many expected the Prince Regent to intervene in favour of those who plotted against the Prime Minister, Spencer Perceval. The Prince, who had only just received full legal power to act as the de facto monarch, decided not to replace Perceval.

THURSDAY 25th FEBRUARY 1993

The Brighton & Hove Leader reported that Brighton's gay and lesbian lonely hearts were planning to storm auditions for ITV's *Blind Date* being held in the town. "Their move is in response to what they say is discrimination against them by the programme, which has never featured a gay or lesbian couple. The protesters have even dubbed the programme *Blind Prejudice*. The anger stems from a series of letters sent to the show by Chris Mills, who is gay. He says he has written to the producer three times in the past four years, but has never received a reply. "The researchers of *Blind Date* come to Brighton, the gay capital of the country, and just ignore us," he told the *Leader* ...

BRIGHTON'S JUBILEE LIBRARY WAS OPENED IN 2005 BY THE PRINCESS ROYAL. © ALAN WARES

... "London Weekend Television should welcome this chance to exercise their equal opportunities policy. The show has been totally heterosexual…" LWT says the auditions at Hospitality Inn, are "open to everyone from all walks of life…" *The Leader* used to be one of the twin towns' most popular newspapers and, as at 2012, is essentially just a big advert.

WEDNESDAY 26th FEBRUARY 1958

Major Carlo Campbell died aged 70 at the Sussex County Hospital. A fighter pilot in World War I, the Brighton & Hove Albion chairman – held in high esteem across the country – had been advised to slow down by his doctors. His deputy, Alec Whitcher, told the *Brighton & Hove Herald*; "The major's death is a grievous blow to us all."

SATURDAY 27th FEBRUARY 1960

Comedian Tony Hawks was born in Brighton. Educated in the town, he shot to fame as leader of the trio Morris Minor & the Majors and reached number four in the UK charts with the Beastie Boys parody, *Stutter Rap (No Sleep Til Bedtime)* in 1988. He's written five books including *One Hit Wonderland* which describes his attempt – over ten years after his first – to write a second hit song. It culminates in him performing on Albanian television with Norman Wisdom and Tim Rice. He is often confused for the famous skateboarder Tony Hawk and once appeared on *Celebrity Mastermind* using the American as his chosen specialised subject. Hawks noted that his correspondents "might be able to do backside aerials but they can't spell to save their lives".

FRIDAY 28th FEBRUARY 1890

Apparently capable of taking up to ten photographs per second using perforated celluloid film, a report on William Friese-Greene's 'chronophotographic' camera was published in the *British Photographic News*. Working in Brighton, he experimented with a system known as Biocolour. In 1921, Friese-Greene was attending a film and cinema industry meeting in London to discuss the poor state of the British film industry. Disturbed by the tone of the proceedings, Friese-Greene got to his feet to speak but soon became incoherent, was helped to his seat, and shortly after, slumped forward and died.

FRIDAY 29th FEBRUARY 1980

A Hove man was cleared of stealing 13,500 books and 400 LPs, despite the items being found stacked in piles in his Ventnor Villas flat. His defence said there was no evidence to suggest that the building's sole occupant, 76-year-old Reginald Patterson, had taken the books and records. Other than them all being discovered in his flat, your honour.

MARCH

FRIDAY 1st MARCH 1839

Sussex County Cricket Club was formally constituted on this day. The club have won three County Championships, in 2003, 2006 and 2007, and are the oldest cricket club in England.

MONDAY 2nd MARCH 1931

Varndean Sixth-Form College, the boys' municipal secondary school, was opened by Viscount Hailsham to replace the Pelham Street Boys School; both later became grammar schools.

THURSDAY 3rd MARCH 2005

The Jubilee Library opened on World Book Day. The innovative glass-fronted structure is one of the most successful public libraries in the country and attracts nearly a million visits every year, issuing over 500,000 items. The centrepiece of the city's £50m Jubilee Square development – winner of 14 awards since opening – the building was designed to take advantage of natural energy provided by its south coast setting; specifically sunshine and wind. The sun's energy is gathered through the vast glass south wall and the heat is stored in walls and a specially constructed floor, being released slowly into surrounding spaces as part of a low energy release ventilation and heating system. The toilets are flushed with recovered rainwater.

SATURDAY 3rd MARCH 2007

Whitehawk Football Club's FA Vase dream ended amid controversy on and off the pitch at a packed East Brighton Park. Visitors Truro City clinched a place in the semi-finals but Hawks were convinced the referee should have disallowed the goal for handball. A crowd of 1,009 saw manager and former Albion player Ian Chapman step in to restrain irate supporters as the Cornish outfit scored a hotly disputed winner just four minutes from time.

MONDAY 4th MARCH 2002

The Argus reported Brighton Bears' biggest win of the season, a 125-98 thrashing of Derby Storm at the Thunderdome.

THURSDAY 5th MARCH 2009

The Argus reported on the disturbing number of public houses going out of business in Sussex. Brighton and Hove has always had more than its fair share of boozers. Inns, taverns and ale-houses have been regulated from at least 1618, and by 1800 there were 41 establishments recorded in the town. The Beer Act of 1830 permitted any ratepayer to open a beer-house on payment of two guineas. The enterprising Brightonians wasted no time and 100 were licensed in the first week! By 1879, there were 424 public houses, and in 1889 there were reported to be 774, one for every 130 residents. A hundred years later there were 235 public houses in Brighton (not including Hove), one for every 600 inhabitants. In 1931, North Road alone had ten pubs.

FRIDAY 6th MARCH 1846

Renowned dermatologist Henry Radcliffe Crocker was born in Hove. At a meeting of the Pathological Society of London in 1885, Crocker was the first to put forward a theory on the condition of Joseph Merrick, known as the Elephant Man, suggesting the condition was caused by a combination of dermatolysis and bone deformities, as a result of changes in his nervous system.

SATURDAY 7th MARCH 2009

The Justin Fashanu All-Stars football team was launched at a special event in Brighton, supported by the FA. Named after the openly gay striker who killed himself almost 11 years earlier the side – open to gay or straight footballers – played its first fixtures at the Gay Football Supporters Network five-a-side tournament in Yorkshire. Jason Hall, from the Justin Campaign, commented; "We decided that the best thing to do was to have a campaigning football team so the football does the talking. Hopefully [we'll] change people's opinions of gay people on the pitch."

THURSDAY 8th MARCH 1923

African World reported that diamond cutting was likely to resume in Brighton. An agreement was to be signed at the Treasury to ensure disabled soldiers could continue in the work that had begun in 1917. By 1921, Sir Bernard Oppenheimer was employing 2,000 men and when he died in early 1923, the directors examined the business, decided it was unsatisfactory and closed it down, throwing 250 diamond cutters out of work. The expected resumption of activity was largely due to the strenuous efforts of the Ministry of Labour and others interested in the enterprise on behalf of the disabled men.

WEDNESDAY 8th MARCH 1939

Brighton Rugby Club celebrated their 70th anniversary with a match against Rosslyn Park at Preston Park. Unfortunately, the Londoners ...

... ran out 16-0 winners. A post-match banquet and dance took place at the Royal Pavilion.

WEDNESDAY 9th MARCH 1892

British writer and publisher David Garnett was born in Brighton. He is famous for writing the novel *Aspects of Love* (1955), on which the later Andrew Lloyd-Webber musical was based.

MONDAY 10th MARCH 1969

Musical film *Oh! What a Lovely War*, based on the stage musical of the same name, enjoyed its UK release. The celluloid version transferred the mise-en-scene – 'placing on stage', an expression used to describe the design aspects of a theatre or film production, which essentially means 'visual theme' or 'telling a story' – completely into the cinema, with elaborate sequences shot at the West Pier, elsewhere in Brighton, and on the South Downs. The film about World War I – which stars John Mills, John Gielgud, Laurence Olivier, Michael Redgrave, Maggie Smith and Susannah York – portrays the 'Game of War' and focuses mainly on the members of the Smith family who go off to war. Much of the action revolves around the words of the soldiers' marching songs.

SUNDAY 10th MARCH 1974

Power cuts brought the country to its knees. Albion – trying to increase gate revenue – hosted only their second-ever Sunday match; a Third Division 2-1 win over Hereford United. It worked as 17,061 fans turned up, compared to the season's average of 10,848.

FRIDAY 11th MARCH 1932

A resident of Brunswick Square, Hove, had a letter published in *The Times*: "Sir, – as a resident of Hove I crave your powerful support to draw attention to the Hove Pier Bill, due to come up for second reading in the House of Lords immediately which, if passed, would destroy our residential amenities for all time by the erection of a pier. 'Floreat Hova' is the motto used by as so far Hove flourishes, it is mainly due to the peaceful enjoyment by its inarticulate residents of a glorious and uninterrupted sea frontage. It is therefore astounding that the corporation, the rightful defenders of the residents, should abstain from opposition in such a vital matter and should connive at the erection of a pier at all. They appear to content themselves with the protective clause which, in effect, is silent as to use after the pier, with all its appurtenances has been erected... but the advent of a pier is calculated to lessen rather than increase the residential attractions of Hove and damage property values... No case of necessity for the establishment of another pier can be sustained, nor even 'public advantage' as cited in the preamble of the Bill, for Brighton's seafront, which merges into Hove, already provides two well-equipped piers... I suggest that all interested residents of Hove should write to their Parliamentary representative on the subject, and I appeal to members of the Legislature to protect Hove's undoubted rights to a tranquil and unspoilt seafront against speculative encroachments such as are embodied in the measure. I have the honour to be, Sir. Your obedient servant, Cecil B Levita."

SATURDAY 12th MARCH 1983

The Goldstone Ground was full to its 28,000 capacity for the visit of Norwich City... in the FA Cup sixth round. It was the furthest the Albion had ever progressed in the competition and the excitement in the twin towns was almost at fever pitch! Jimmy Case had netted in the previous three rounds and it was the Liverpudlian who fired the Albion to a semi-final date with Sheffield Wednesday at Highbury. Andy Ritchie flicked on for the midfielder to muscle past the Canaries' defence to slot past future England keeper Chris Woods in front of an ecstatic North Stand.

MONDAY 13th MARCH 1978

Vaultage 78, a compilation album of Brighton's punk bands, was released. Only a thousand copies of the vinyl LP were pressed that introduced one of the town's newest bands to the unsuspecting Sussex public – Peter and the Test Tube Babies. The four-piece punk outfit were formed in a Peacehaven garage in the same year and were soon touring the world with their unashamedly non-serious songs in 'Punk Pathetique' – a subgenre of British punk rock (circa 1980-1982) involving humour and working-class cultural themes. Still going strong over 30 years later, the group have launched such timeless classics as *Pissed and Proud* (1982), *Mating Sounds of South American Frogs* (1983), *Journey to the Centre of Johnny Clarke's Head* (1984), *Soberphobia* (1986), *The $hit Factory* (1990), *Supermodels* (1995) and *A Foot Full of Bullets* (2005). And, let's not forget the ground-breaking singles; *The Queen Gives Good Blow Jobs* (1982), and *Rotting in the Fart Sack EP* (1985).

THURSDAY 14th MARCH 1844

The first Chief Constable of Brighton Borough Police, Henry Solomon, died from the head injuries he received after being bludgeoned with a poker while interviewing a prisoner. In 1836, six years after a police ...

... force was first established in Brighton – to replace the watchmen system – Solomon became its Chief Constable, a post he served for eight years, until the day he died. His office was in the Town Hall and one day, when he was interrogating young John Lawrence about his part in the theft of a roll of carpeting from a shop, the 23-year-old suspect attacked. He was left alone for a moment and seized the opportunity to grab a poker from the fireplace to strike Solomon on the head. The blow was hard enough to bend the poker. Lawrence was arrested, convicted and then hanged at Lewes Prison. Queen Victoria donated £50 towards an appeal to raise funds for the welfare of Solomon's widow and nine children. He is thought to be the only chief constable in the UK to have been murdered in his own police station and his ghost reputedly haunts the basement of the office buildings. Buried in Brighton's Florence Place Old Jewish Burial Ground – and featured on a Brighton & Hove Bus – Solomon's gravestone inscription reads; "15 years chief officer of police| of the town of Brighton| who was brutally murdered| while in the public discharge| of the duties of his office| on the 14th day of March 1844| in the fiftieth year of his age." In 1810 eight 'watchmen' were appointed to patrol the town at night with another 16 recruited by December 1815. In January 1821, the town was divided into eight watch districts, each with a box for the watchman. The watchmen were dressed in top hats, black tail-coats and white trousers, and were armed with batons and rattles.

MONDAY 15th MARCH 1937

Tommy Farr became British and Empire heavyweight champion. One of the most famous Welsh and British boxers of all time, 'the Tonypandy Terror' fought world heavyweight champion Joe Louis at Yankee Stadium, New York City, five months later and gained respect from the 50,000 crowd, who booed when Louis was awarded a narrow points decision. On retirement, Farr ran the Royal Standard pub in Queen's Road, Brighton.

THURSDAY 16th MARCH 1826

Thirteen years earlier, a fund was started for the establishment of a hospital in the town, but nothing materialised until December 1824 when a meeting at the Old Ship resolved to construct a county hospital. Architect Charles Barry was commissioned to design the new building – to be built on land donated by Thomas Kemp – and the foundation stone was laid by the Earl of Egremont on this day. The Sussex County Hospital and General Sea-Bathing Infirmary opened just over two years later on June 11th 1828 with four large, and 23 small, wards ...

KING'S ROAD, BRIGHTON IN THE 1950S, LOOKING EAST TOWARDS THE WEST PIER AND, IN THE DISTANCE, THE PALACE PIER

... providing room for 80 patients. Sea-water treatment was then considered very important and water was pumped through a pipe from the beach. The practice ceased in 1876.

SUNDAY 16th MARCH 1862

Four years earlier a well was started at the Warren Farm Industrial School – home to 300 children – in Warren Road, Brighton. The aim of the facility was to teach the misplaced youth of the town 'the habits of industry' and relieve them from 'the bane of pauperism'. The expense of having pumped water supplied from the local waterworks, then on the corner of Lewes Road (now Saunders Park), was considered prohibitive, so it was decided to construct a single well; initially a six-feet wide, brick-lined shaft down some 400 feet to the subterranean water table. After two years of digging, the workers had only reached a depth of some 438 feet, but no water had been found. A lateral chamber was constructed 30 feet away, to no avail. Further lateral tunnels were driven westwards and eastwards, again without hitting the jackpot. A further four-foot wide shaft was sanctioned at the end of the eastern tunnel and digging continued 24-hours-a-day by candlelight. In appalling conditions many workers worked naked; within the confines of a four-foot circle teams of men had to dig, load buckets and lay bricks. Winchmen stood on tiny platforms cut into the side of the shaft, passing spoil up and bricks down. The Woodingdean Well was costing the local ratepayer £90 a week and the natives were getting restless. At the change of evening shifts on this day, a bricklayer noticed that the thin crust of earth he was standing on was being slowly pushed upwards like a giant piston. At such a depth it would take 45 minutes of rapid ascent to reach the ground! Scrambling up the numerous ladders to get to the winchman's platform, he and the others quickly vacated the shaft. Suddenly with a roar, tools, buckets and ladders were jettisoned. Water at last! Four years of hard toil to hand-dig a shaft some 1,285 feet deep – 850 of which were below sea level – without the aid of machines. An amazing achievement.

SATURDAY 17th MARCH 2007

A march through Brighton city centre by 40 campaigners defending the right to protest, passed peacefully. The demonstration was organised by Sussex Action for Peace as a response to over-zealous policing at a march against Israel's attack on Lebanon the previous year.

TUESDAY 18th MARCH 1947

The UK release date for *Brighton Rock*. Based on the novel of the same name by Graham Greene, the film centres on the activities of a gang of assorted criminals and, in particular, their leader – the vicious 'Pinkie'. The film focuses on the criminal underbelly of inter-war Brighton. Pinkie orders the murder of a rival, Fred, and the police believe it to be suicide. This doesn't convince Ida Arnold, who was with Fred just before he died, and she sets out to discover the truth. She meets naive waitress Rose, who can prove that Fred was murdered. In an attempt to keep Rose quiet Pinkie marries her as his gang begins to doubt his ability and his rivals start to take over his business. Pinkie becomes more desperate and violent...

FRIDAY 19th MARCH 1999

A town in Berkshire, 50 miles away from the sea, decided to promote itself as an alternative seaside resort to Brighton and Hove! Bracknell shipped in hundreds of tonnes of sand to transform part of the town centre into a beach complete with sand dunes, palm trees, deck chairs and Punch & Judy shows, alongside the more traditional concrete attractions. Was it a success? Answers on a postcard...

TUESDAY 20th MARCH 1945

Lord Alfred Douglas died in Lancing. His early poetry was Uranian – a 19th century term referring to a person of a third sex, originally, someone with 'a female psyche in a male body' who is sexually attracted to men – and he was well known as the lover of the writer Oscar Wilde. While staying together in Brighton, Douglas fell ill with influenza and was nursed back to health by Wilde, but failed to return the favour when Wilde fell ill.

FRIDAY 21st MARCH 1990

Seminal dance music anthem *Chime*, by Orbital, was at number 18 in the UK pop charts. The group comprised the Hartnoll brothers, Paul and Phil, who is a long-term Brighton resident.

THURSDAY 22nd MARCH 1973

Brighton Council unanimously rejected the 'Wilson report', a town-centre plan that proposed large-scale road construction in the Preston Circus area and a 'spine road' through the North Laine to a car park in Church Street. Both plans involved the demolition of over 500 houses, simply as an interim measure! More were proposed. Five conservation areas were designated that year with five more in 1977, most notably North Laine. Imagine if the plan had got the green light? A sobering thought indeed.

THURSDAY 22nd MARCH 1990

A landmark evening for the late-night revellers of the twin towns; Busby's nightclub reopened as Oriana's, while the adjacent Top Rank Suite was renamed The Event. The latter, in particular, is responsible for many a Brightonian's birth!

FRIDAY 23rd MARCH 1832

The Brighton Gazette alluded to a piece in *The Times*: "700 persons have died of small-pox in Brighton, in a population of 40,000 souls, in about the same time that cholera, though pretty widely spread, has destroyed not quite 1,800, out of a population of several millions."

SATURDAY 24th MARCH 1973

Tricia Burtenshaw was crowned Miss Albion at the Brighton & Hove Albion Supporters' Club dance at the Arlington Hotel.

SUNDAY 25th MARCH 2001

Table tennis in Brighton received a boost in the form of a £4,200 cheque from the national Awards for All scheme. The 100-strong Brighton Community League was now recognised and affiliated to the Brighton League, the Sussex Table Tennis Association and the English Table Tennis Association. Unfortunately, it wasn't all good news as the All-Sussex Senior Championships was lost to Horsham.

FRIDAY 26th MARCH 1976

The world's first Body Shop opened at 22 Kensington Gardens in North Laine. On this day, according to folklore, the company's founder, Anita Roddick, had the bright idea of dripping strawberry bath oil from Western Road right to the door of her new premises. It soon worked and the shop became very busy! The original store had just 15 products – compared to over 300 nowadays. There are now 2,400 stores in 61 countries.

MONDAY 27th MARCH 1837

Long-time companion of Royal Pavilion resident George, Prince of Wales, Maria Fitzherbert died aged 80 at Steine House. Maria married Edward Weld, a rich Catholic landowner of Lulworth Castle, 16 years her senior, in July 1775. Weld died just three months later after a fall from his horse and having failed to sign his new will his estate went to his younger brother Thomas leaving Maria effectively destitute. She needed to re-marry, and quick. Three years later she became Mrs

Fitzherbert and her husband Thomas died in 1781; she inherited a Mayfair house and £2,500-a-year (£125,000 in today's money). The young widow soon entered London high society and in spring 1784 she was introduced to a youthful George. They married in December of the following year but their union was considered invalid under the Royal Marriages Act (1772) as it had not been approved by King George III and the Privy Council. Had permission been asked, it would probably not have been granted as Mrs Fitzherbert was a Roman Catholic. They continued their romance even after the Prince's marriage to Caroline of Brunswick, and the Prince returned to live with Maria in about 1800, but their relationship had ended permanently by 1811. The new King, William IV, offered her a dukedom after George's death in 1830 as recompense for the difficulties she had suffered on his brother's behalf. Architect William Porden designed Steine House, on the west side of Old Steine, and she lived there from 1804 until her death.

SATURDAY 27th MARCH 1976

A memorable day in the history of Brighton & Hove Albion Football Club: manager Peter Taylor decided to bring on a slightly-built 20-year-old forward to replace leading scorer Fred Binney at league leaders Hereford United. With his first touch, on his Albion debut, Peter Ward netted to level the score. A legend was born...

FRIDAY 28th MARCH 2003

A huge fire raged through what was remaining of the West Pier. It started at 9.45am and smoke had engulfed Hove by mid-afternoon. There was a suspicion of arson which the police dismissed after interviewing people seen in a speedboat in the area around the time the blaze began. The pier – built in 1866 – had been in a state of disrepair for many years and has been closed to the public since 1975. In February 2003 a £30m scheme to restore the derelict structure was approved by councillors at Brighton and Hove City Council. The fire left just the metal skeleton of the derelict pier standing.

TUESDAY 29th MARCH 2007

Community radio station Radio Reverb was awarded an FM licence. Offering an eclectic mix of information, views, arts and music from around the world and presented by the people of Brighton and Hove – with no adverts or agenda – the station offers the broadest content of any broadcaster in the south-east. An excellent example of what makes Brighton great.

TUESDAY 30th MARCH 1880

Named after the hundred-eyed all-seeing giant of Greek mythology, *The Argus* was published at 130 North Street where a loft on the roof housed the pigeons that brought in stories from the far corners of the county. Initially costing one halfpenny, the paper was renamed the *Evening Argus* on January 1st 1897. The price increased to a penny in 1918 and the first photograph – of a fire at the Court Theatre in New Road – was printed in February 1926. In the same year, Southern Publishing acquired Robinson's printing works and adjoining premises at the southern end of Robert Street, which enabled all departments to be housed in the same building. Circulation reached 100,000 – it had been as low as 19,000 during World War II – in October 1964, and was around 250,000 by 1990. The paper went completely 'electronic' in 1987 and moved to a £20 million newspaper printing facility at the Hollingbury industrial estate in 1993.

THURSDAY 31st MARCH 1898

Eleanor Marx, sixth daughter of the revolutionary Karl, sent her maid to the local chemist for chloroform and a small quantity of prussic acid (hydrogen cyanide) – for 'the dog' – and ended her life, aged 43. A socialist like her father, she had discovered that her ailing partner, Edward Aveling, had secretly married a young actress. Aveling's illness seemed to her to be terminal and she became deeply depressed by the faithlessness of the man she loved. On this fateful day, she wrote two brief suicide notes, undressed, got into bed, and swallowed the poison. There's a blue plaque, commemorating her residence, at 6 Vernon Terrace, Brighton.

APRIL

SATURDAY 1st APRIL 1854

Brighton was incorporated as a borough. The boundary followed the present border with Hove from the seafront, via Little Western Street and Boundary Passage to Goldsmid Road and on to the junctions of Russell Crescent and Dyke Road, and Prestonville Road and Old Shoreham Road. From here, it followed the line of Old Shoreham Road, New England Road, Viaduct Road, Ditchling Road, Florence Place, Hollingdean Road and Bear Road to the Race Hill to encompass an area of approximately 1,640 acres. Exactly 74 years later in 1928 the borough of Hove was extended to include Hangleton, most of West Blatchington and part of Patcham, bringing the total area to 3,953 acres. Also included was the village of Ovingdean – the 'valley of Ofa's people' – that was described in the *Domesday Book* of 1086 as a manor held by Godfrey de Pierpoint. A possible victim of an attack by the French raiders who terrorised Rottingdean in 1377, Ovingdean's population had risen to about 1,000 by 1981. Forty-six years later – to the day – under the 1972 Local Government Act, Portslade-by-Sea was merged into the new borough of Hove with the urban parishes abolished.

TUESDAY 1st APRIL 1952

Originally known as 'Cold Dean', the north-eastern suburb of Coldean officially became part of the borough of Brighton. In 1990, the largest site of Bronze Age huts in Sussex was found on the south-western side of Coldean Lane where the bypass was constructed.

WEDNESDAY 1st APRIL 1964

Paul Guppy rescued six people from the burning Bedford Hotel on Brighton seafront. The 19-year-old from Rottingdean ran into the hotel when he heard screams and discovered them huddled in a corner. "I led five out through an emergency exit. Then I went back in and carried out an old lady."

TUESDAY 1st APRIL 1980

Saggy bellies, knobbly knees and unflattering angles were exposed as Brighton's infamous naturist beach was opened at the Cliff bathing area below Duke's Mound – the first on a prime beach at a British resort. In 1807, the parish prohibited bathing without a machine between Royal Crescent and the brick kilns at the Hove boundary. John Crunden was fined for bathing naked in 1809.

SUNDAY 2nd APRIL 1989

Brighton Pavilion MP Julian Amery cut the first turf of the Brighton and Hove bypass in the Waterhall Valley. Running for 8.5 miles – from the Shoreham bypass, just west of the Kingston roundabout, to the Lewes Road at Stanmer Park – the road was to be part of the A27 Folkestone to Honiton trunk road.

WEDNESDAY 2nd APRIL 2008

The Royal Mint officially announced that production of Matthew Dent's coins was now underway at its Llantrisant HQ. The 26-year-old from Gwynedd, who completed a graphic design degree at the University of Brighton in 2003, beat 4,000 entries in a competition to revamp the country's coins; from the penny to the pound. The Welshman, who won the £35,000 prize after receiving an email from a friend, said; "From a forwarded website link, to a piece of art in everyone's pocket, it has been a fascinating journey, an education, and thoroughly enjoyable."

MONDAY 3rd APRIL 1826

The Brighton Herald reported: "Nearly 100 persons have been summoned in Brighton, this week, for non-payment of their poor rates; and between 30 and 40 distress warrants have, we regret to state, been issued against defaulters, some of whom have been accustomed to move in a respectable sphere of life."

FRIDAY 4th APRIL 1823

Bricklayer Daniel Watts and sawyer James Smith competed in a famous prize fight. Contested in Ovingdean, as it was just outside the borough of Brighton and away from the police, a ring was roped out and the bout commenced just before 4pm. After more than an hour Smith was knocked unconscious – he died the next morning. Watts was charged with manslaughter but passed away from his own injuries before he could be brought to trial.

SATURDAY 5th APRIL 2003

Brighton Cougars lost 88-58 at their Liverpool basketball counterparts. Coach Mike Blatchford lamented; "Whether it was the long bus trip, the lousy officiating, intimidation or the gods of basketball, we stunk. We missed 24 free throws, I don't know how many lay-ups and just got walloped."

SATURDAY 6th APRIL 1974

As a result of Luxembourg's brace of wins in the preceding years, the BBC stepped in to host the Eurovision Song Contest at The Dome. Inspired by the growing glam rock scene in England, 'The Abba' made their television debut singing *Waterloo*. The Swedish four-piece – Agnetha, Benny, Björn and Anni-Frid – won with the least percentage of votes, 15%, ever recorded; a record that stands unbeaten over 38 years later. In 1974, the voting rules were completely different to the current system as each country had just ten jurors, who gave one vote apiece to their favourite song. Of the ten points available to distribute, the UK gave five to Italy, two to Israel and one each to Finland, Ireland and Switzerland, and none to the Swedes. The UK's entry, sung by Cambridge-born Olivia Newton John, finished fourth with *Long Live Love*. The Abba collected 24 points, Italy (18) – the UK panel awarded Gigliola Cinquetti a maximum five points – Netherlands (15) and the UK (14). No country had to endure the ignominy of 'nul points' but Norway, West Germany and Switzerland, respectively, shared the wooden spoon with three points each. Fast forward to January 2010 and two members of one of the biggest-selling groups of all time admitted they were completely unaware that the UK had given them a big, fat zero. "All these years and I thought the Brits were our best friends," joked Bjorn.

SATURDAY 7th APRIL 2007

The Argus reported on a setback for the return of the tuc-tucs. The three-wheeled people carriers – a common sight in Thailand and the Far East – were introduced to Brighton and Hove's streets in July 2006 and proved so popular their fleet doubled from 12 vehicles in the first month. On this day, the tuc-tucs were banned from making their spring comeback due to a series of blunders by licensing officials. TucTuc Ltd director Dominic Ponniah said; "It is TucTuc Ltd that has been left to pay the price for the complete disorganisation, arrogance and shameless chaos of the traffic commissioner's office."

MONDAY 8th APRIL 2002

The BBC website reported that a 14-year-old boy from Brighton was recovering in hospital after a police dog bit off part of his ear. The teenager had to undergo a six-hour operation to re-attach the lobe of his right ear, bitten off after a fight in Morley Street two days earlier.

THE *ATHINA B*, WHICH RAN AGROUND IN 1980

SUNDAY 9th APRIL 1876

Alf Sharp, the first professional footballer signed by a Brighton club, was born in the town. The inside-forward played for Brighton United before joining the Albion in 1901. He made just one appearance, against Shepherd's Bush.

TUESDAY 9th APRIL 1940

Now three huge – and largely soulless – retail units, 134 North Street opened as the 1,877-seater Imperial Theatre. The Art Deco auditorium became The Essoldo in 1950 and closed 14 years later. The last pictures shown were *Never Let Go* and *Teenage Lovers*. A Top Rank bingo hall emerged which was converted into a youth-oriented entertainment complex called Hot Shots, complete with a bowling alley, in 1997. The venue lasted just two years and, after a failed attempt to get the building listed in 1999, the site was demolished.

FRIDAY 9th APRIL 1948

Brighton Tigers fans flew to Nottingham, from Shoreham, for an away fixture. The supporters' trip – 21 travelled in all – was organised by 'cheerleader' Charlie Connell.

MONDAY 9th APRIL 2001

Staff and shoppers ran for cover as a cliff crumbled onto the Brighton Marina Asda store. At around 8.30 am rocks and debris fell into a yard and plunged the bottom-patting supermarket into darkness. A water tanker, used to supply the store's sprinkler system, was knocked over, and an electricity generator cut out. Fire crews and police cordoned off a 300-metre area around the fall while engineers from Brighton & Hove City Council arrived, accompanied by power company workmen. Warehouse manager Paul Medhurst explained; "I heard a loud rumble, just like thunder, and a big bang. We have a freezer at the back and it was moving towards me and I just ran. I've never heard anything like it. It was like an intense breaking of glass and I felt the earth shake."

MONDAY 10th APRIL 1961

The Goldstone Ground switched on its distinctive 'drench lighting' floodlights, which cost £13,523, for the first time in a friendly against champions of Denmark, Boldklubben Frem. Based in the Valby-Sydhavnen area of Copenhagen, the club has won the Danish Championship six times – and the Danish Cup twice – since its foundation in 1886.

FRIDAY 11th APRIL 2003

Tycoon Nicholas Hoogstraten lost his first bid for freedom. Hoogstraten's legal team made an application at London's High Court to secure bail for the jailed millionaire in advance of a full appeal hearing later this year.

SUNDAY 12th APRIL 2009

Bloodgate. One of the most bizarre and embarrassing plots in professional sport unravelled at The Stoop, home of Harlequins Rugby Club, in south-west London. Quins were 5-6 down in the dying minutes of a Heineken Cup quarter-final tie against Leinster and wanted to switch Brighton-born wing/full-back Tom Williams for a specialist kicker. The change was made under the blood injury rule, which permits bleeding players to be removed for treatment. Williams was seen removing a fake blood capsule from his sock, placing it in his mouth and chewing on it before being taken off the field. He then winked broadly towards his team bench as the red substance oozed. Proving that cheats never prosper, the substitute, former All Black fly-half Nick Evans, missed the late goal kick, Harlequins lost, and rugby officials began an inquiry. Coach and former England international Dean Richards was banned from rugby, worldwide, physiotherapist Stephen Brennan was struck off in September 2010, Williams' initial 12-month ban was reduced to four months on appeal and Harlequin Football Club was fined £260,000.

THURSDAY 13th APRIL 2006

A tomato that could help reduce the risk of developing cancer went on sale, reported the finger-on-the-pulse *Argus*. A large supermarket launched a new variety of the fruit containing a third more lycopene; the pigment which gives tomatoes their red colour, and a powerful antioxidant.

FRIDAY 14th APRIL 2006

The Brighton Bears played their last ever game of professional basketball at Newcastle Eagles. The club was formed in 1973 by Dave Goss and initially consisted of a part-time squad of locals who played in the County League. Four years later the Bears took the step up to play in the National League Division Two and were in the top flight in 1981. High rents precipitated a move to Worthing in 1984. A 15-year tenure along the coast, including a championship in 1993, ended with a return to home games at the Brighton Centre and Burgess Hill's Triangle – regularly attracting crowds of up to 3,000 – in 1999. Another title followed in 2004 before Nick Nurse and his fellow directors pulled the plug in 2006.

TUESDAY 15th APRIL 1958

Extremist cleric Abu Hamza al-Masri – famous for his hook hand and incendiary speeches at the controversial Finsbury Park mosque in north London – was born in Alexandria, Egypt. The son of a middle-class army officer, who once allegedly proclaimed Britain as "a paradise, where you could do anything you wanted", studied civil engineering at Brighton Polytechnic.

SATURDAY 16th APRIL 1983

Hundreds on coaches departed from the Greyhound Stadium for the FA Cup semi-final at Highbury! Albion had avoided Manchester United and Arsenal and were drawn against Sheffield Wednesday. Jimmy Case continued his goalscoring run by smashing a 35-yard free kick against the underside of the crossbar, and in, to give the Albion a 14th-minute lead. Yugoslav international midfielder Ante Mirocevic scrambled home an equaliser on 57 minutes before Michael Robinson swivelled and shot with 12 minutes remaining to fire the Seagulls to Wembley for the first time in their 82-year history!

MONDAY 17th APRIL 1786

Dr William King was a physician and philanthropist from Brighton. He was an early supporter of the Co-operative Movement – a co-operative (co-op) is a business organisation owned and operated by a group of individuals for their mutual benefit – and in 1827 the idea was taken to the United States. He opened a store in Brighton and a year later founded *The Co-operator* to promote the ideas. King's rationale for the movement is best illustrated by the phrases on the masthead of every issue: 'Knowledge and union are power. Power, directed by knowledge is happiness. Happiness is the end of creation'.

MONDAY 17th APRIL 1933

It's announced that Brighton Council will discuss the demolition of the Clock Tower at their next meeting. A gift from James Welling, the structure was erected in 1888. *The Times* reported; "Though frequently seen as inartistic and an obstruction, the tower has hitherto been allowed to remain but now, in view of modern traffic conditions and the narrow roadway which the tower creates, its removal is being sought by some… One prominent member of the council said: The Clock Tower is both hideous and an obstruction. It must make way for modern Brighton… We suggest its demolition and the use of the debris for road metal. The Clock Tower has many champions among residents and visitors, who regard it as one of the main features of Brighton, but the demands of modern traffic are likely to win the day..."

SUNDAY 18th APRIL 2010

The first Brighton Marathon. The road race, run over the distance of 42.195 km or 26 miles and 385 yards, was organised by former international athlete Tim Hutchings and former Brighton club athlete, Tom Naylor. Of the original 12,000 applicants, 7,589 runners were present on the start line at Preston Park as former Olympian – and Brightonian – Steve Ovett officially started the race. The route took in central Brighton before heading east towards along the front to Rottingdean, back west out to, and around – effectively lapping the flat and straight New Church Road – Hove, before returning on the seafront and finishing on Madeira Drive, close to the Palace Pier. The Guardian's DD Guttenplan was supposed to be running the 103rd Boston Marathon too but was scuppered by the Eyjafjallajökull ash cloud in Iceland: "I'd still like to run Boston... but with such a great race so close to home, I'd strongly suggest anyone crowded out of London – or simply in the mood for a change – consider taking the train to the pain." The inaugural victors were Mongolian SerOd 'Ziggy' Bat-Ochir, in the men's race with a time of 2:19:05, and Brit Jo Bryce in the women's race (3:05:20).

SUNDAY 19th APRIL 1953

The Portuguese release date for the film *Genevieve*, three months before its UK launch. The British comedy features two couples and revolves around two Brass Era cars and their crews participating in the annual London to Brighton Veteran Car Run. Alan McKim, a young barrister, and his wife Wendy drive Genevieve, a 1904 Darracq – while their friend Ambrose Claverhouse, a brash advertising salesman, his latest girlfriend, fashion model Rosalind Peters and her pet St Bernard, ride in a 1904 Spyker. The journey to Brighton goes well for Claverhouse, but the McKims' trip is complicated by several breakdowns, and they arrive very late. As Alan cancelled their accommodation in their usual plush hotel, they are forced to spend the night in a run-down establishment leaving Wendy somewhat upset. They finally join Ambrose and Rosalind for after-dinner drinks, but Rosalind gets very drunk and insists on playing the trumpet with the house band – which she does surprisingly well, giving a spirited rendition of the song *Genevieve*, before passing out. Alan and Wendy argue over Ambrose's supposed romantic attentions to her, and Alan goes off to the garage to sulk. Whilst working on his car in the middle of the night, Ambrose turns up. Angry words are ...

... exchanged and Alan impulsively bets Ambrose £100 that he can beat him back to London – despite racing not being allowed by the club. Ambrose accepts: "First over Westminster Bridge." Despite Rosalind's massive hangover, and Wendy's determined disapproval of the whole business, the two crews race back to London. Both cars are stopped by traffic police and are warned after Alan and Ambrose come to blows. At Wendy's insistence, they call off the bet and decide to have a party instead. This idea is soon cancelled; while waiting for the pub to open, words are exchanged and the bet is on again. The two cars race neck-and-neck through the southern suburbs of London and with only a few yards to go, Genevieve breaks down. As Ambrose's car is about to overtake, its tyres become stuck in tramlines and it drives off in another direction. The brakes on Genevieve fail and the car rolls a few yards onto Westminster Bridge – thus winning the bet.

THURSDAY 20th APRIL 1939

Ray Brooks was born in Brighton. Famous as the voice of *Mr Benn*, he has appeared in *Coronation Street* and starred in the award-winning 1965 documentary *Cathy Come Home*. A number of small roles followed, including *The Avengers* and a period of predominantly voiceover work in the 1970s, before a return to form with BBC series *Big Deal*, a comedy/drama about the ups and downs of poker addict Robbie Box. In 2006, he did the whole country a favour when his character, Joe Macer, killed perpetual misery Pauline Fowler in *EastEnders*. His son, Will, founded MyFootballClub in 2008. The group of 50,000 fans, paying £35 each, purchased Ebbsfleet United, a professional football club, and voted on decisions.

THURSDAY 21st APRIL 1814

Angela Georgina Burdett-Coutts, 1st Baroness Burdett-Coutts was born. In 1837 she became the wealthiest woman in England when she inherited her grandfather's fortune of nearly £3million. She collected significant paintings and became a notable subject of public curiosity, receiving numerous offers of marriage. Famous for throwing large parties at The Holly Lodge in Highgate, which was then just outside London, Burdett-Coutts spent part of each year at the Royal Albion Hotel in Brighton with her companion Hannah. She spent the majority of her wealth on scholarships, endowments, and a wide range of philanthropic causes and one of her earliest donations was to establish, with her friend Charles Dickens, Urania Cottage, a home that helped young women who had 'turned to a life of immorality' to escape from prostitution Burdett-Coutts helped a huge array of good causes including the British

Beekeepers Association, RSPCA, St Paul's Cathedral, Turkish refugees, Aborigines, The Temperance Society, British Horological Institute, and many, many more. She also founded Columbia Road market in 1869 in Bethnal Green, London. When Hannah died in 1878, Burdett-Coutts wrote to a friend that she was utterly crushed by the loss of "my poor darling, the companion and sunshine of my life for 52 years". She shocked polite society by marrying her 29-year-old secretary, William Lehman Ashmead Bartlett, the American-born MP for Westminster, three years later at the age of 67. An amazing woman.

MONDAY 22nd APRIL 1822

Home to temporary auditoriums during the Brighton Festival, a fountain, thousands of pigeons, a public convenience converted into a café and a war memorial, the Old Steine was officially designated as an open space by Thomas Kemp and other landowners on behalf of the town. Known simply as 'The Steine' to locals, the natural focal point of the town became the Old Steine in the 1790s when the New Steine was developed on the East Cliff. It is believed that the name, in use since the 16th century, derived from a Flemish word meaning 'stone' as a number of large sarsen stones have been recovered from the area. For centuries it was an ill-drained, treeless area of grassland, with the intermittent Wellesbourne River flowing down the western side. Brighton fishermen used the area for drying nets and storing boats in bad weather and in 1665 it was said to include a bowling green and extend beyond East Street. In 1760, the town's first library opened on the eastern side and in 1776, wooden railings were erected to enclose the grassland, much to the anger of the fishermen. The Steine was further improved in 1792/93 when a sewer was constructed along the western side to channel the Wellesbourne and improve the drainage, thus removing the stagnant pool that lay along the north-western edge in front of the Prince's Marine Pavilion. Two large hotels, the Royal York and The Albion, opened on the southern side in the 1820s, facing inland. Many trees, some over 140 years old, were victims of the great storm of October 1987.

THURSDAY 22nd APRIL 1965

Michael Attree, a well-known face – and champion moustache wearer – around Brighton and Hove, was born. 'Atters', a well-spoken 'cad', dresses in classic Edwardian style and is an accomplished artist and writer, enjoying success editing the Whiskerade column in *The Chap* magazine. In 2003, he triumphed at the European Beard & Moustache Championships in Milan.

WEDNESDAY 22nd APRIL 1981

Replacing the Brighton Corporation's first swimming pool that had opened in 1895, the Prince Regent's 33-metre pool welcomed its first visitors on this day. The old pool, 120 feet by 33 feet, was initially available to men and women on separate days only and closed in November 1979.

SATURDAY 23rd APRIL 1910

After sitting top of the league since early February, Brighton & Hove Albion won their first championship beating Swindon Town, their closest rivals, at the Goldstone Ground in front of 11,000 spectators. Bullet Jones netted twice – while local boy Bert Longstaff grabbed the other – to lift the Southern League trophy with a game to spare. *The Argus* reported; "Every preparation was made for the accommodation of a big crowd... Extra seating was provided on the west side, and it was needed... All the ring seats and the open stand rapidly became packed, and still the turnstiles clicked in a way that suggested a harvest of silver for the Albion's exchequer." Over a hundred years later and the club could well be looking at much more than silver...

FRIDAY 24th APRIL 1998

Albion general manager Nick Rowe appealed for local businessmen to help the club during a meeting at the Grand Hotel. Director Martin Perry said the club were confident they would get permission to play temporarily at Withdean Stadium, and that a new ground elsewhere would be the envy of towns and cities throughout the country...

WEDNESDAY 25th APRIL 2007

Sixteen 'Earthship' homes for Brighton seafront were given planning approval by the city council. The buildings were to be constructed using recycled car tyres and are designed to be completely self-sufficient, with power provided by wind turbines and solar panels.

SUNDAY 26th APRIL 1975

What was to become the Brighton Gay Switchboard began at the Open Café, a centre for alternative politics, in Victoria Road. The Brighton Lavender Line started by having just a telephone available in a downstairs room of the café, right next to where people ate and smoked. Advertising proved tricky because *The Argus* was not gay-friendly so ads were placed in alternative news-sheets, pubs, newsagents and telephone boxes, late at night.

THE GOLDSTONE GROUND, HOVE, CIRCA 1910

SATURDAY 26th APRIL 1997

The curtain came down on 95 years of football at the Goldstone Ground. The famous old stadium – loved by thousands across the globe – hosted its final match after being sold to property developers by unscrupulous chairman Bill Archer. Doncaster Rovers were the opponents in conditions rather apt for the occasion; grey, overcast and rainy. A tear-inducing two-minute Last Post was played by a lone trumpeter before the teams emerged. In the directors' box for the first time was chairman-elect Dick Knight, with his colleagues Bob Pinnock and Martin Perry. A scrappy, nervy affair was brought to life in the 16th minute when Albion forward Ian Baird and Rovers defender Darren Moore were sent off for fighting. In the 68th minute, winger Stuart Storer side-footed a volley into the roof of the net after Mark Morris had headed against the Doncaster Rovers bar. The souvenir hunters invaded the pitch on the final whistle after bottom-of-the-table Albion had got the precious three points they required. A point the following Saturday at Hereford would ensure league survival...

SATURDAY 27th APRIL 1996

The natives were getting restless at the Goldstone – for a very good reason. The 'no profit' clause was removed from the club's constitution, meaning the club's home for over 90 years could be sold to Chartwell to line the pockets of the chairman, Bill Archer. No announcement had been made as to where Albion would play their home games the following campaign and, added to the club's relegation to the basement for the first time since 1965, the atmosphere among the 9,852 fans in attendance was one of abject fury. The game lasted just 16 minutes. Thousands of loyal Albion fans invaded the pitch and snapped both crossbars forcing the referee to abandon the fixture. Exacerbated at their club's plight, supporters from across the county had organised the protest in order to gain national media attention – it worked. Two days later, the club announced a deal with Chartwell to lease back the Goldstone Ground for one, last, season...

FRIDAY 28th APRIL 1972

More than 100 enquiries were received by British Rail in Derby regarding the sale of the iconic *Brighton Belle*. Initially believed to be worth around £15,000, experts were confident the train's 15 coaches – taken out of service after 40 years – could fetch ten times that amount.

MONDAY 28th APRIL 2008

After grossing over $300m in its first year at the cinema, *The Golden Compass* was released on DVD in the UK. The film concentrates on the adventures of Lyra Belacqua – played by 13-year-old Brightonian Dakota Blue Richards, making her acting debut – an orphan living in a parallel universe.

THURSDAY 29th APRIL 1982

Charlie Connell, well-known locally for his involvement with the Brighton Tigers ice hockey team, died aged 75, just a year after retiring. Together with fellow supporter Bert Head, he formed the Brighton Tigers Supporters Club on the steps of the Sports Stadium (SS) in West Street. The first game attended by Charlie and an organised supporters club was on October 10th 1946, when the Tigers entertained Wembley Monarchs. The club reached its numerical peak in the immediate post-war years when its membership was almost 2,000. Charlie also spent a season at the Goldstone Ground giving the Albion vocal encouragement. He organised the reception for Jimmy Kelly and Reg Merrifield on their return from the World Ice Hockey Championships in Prague in 1938. Some 10,000 people packed Queen's Road and West Street as the two men were driven in a Daimler from Brighton Station to the SS.

SUNDAY 30th APRIL 1967

The first official *Brighton Festival* came to an end. The inaugural event – with an all-seeing eye as a logo – started 16 days earlier with an international wine festival, a performance from the Warsaw Philharmonic Orchestra, and a gay arts ball at the Metropole that continued until dawn. *The Dance of Death* at the Theatre Royal was a hot ticket but the best bit of the festival – apart from the ten-feet structure fashioned from red, blue, yellow and black plastic globes in Regency Square – was the attempt to paint a huge Union Flag... on the surface of the sea between the piers! The desired dyes were unavailable, so the plan was to simply change the colour of the sea. "The only effect," *The Argus* reported, "was large splodges of fluorescent sickly green, which lasted more than an hour, discolouring the briny." The 'artists' had a spray gun and two five-gallon drums of very concentrated crystals. As they prepared for their masterpiece, the boat hit a wave and a cup of crystals was jettisoned skyward, covering the crew. They all turned green. The top music acts to perform during the fortnight included The Who, Georgie Fame and The Blue Flames, Cleo Laine and The Cream.

MAY

MONDAY 1st MAY 1939

The number 48 trolley bus route, replacing tram route L from Old Steine to Preston Barracks, ran for the first time. A hit with the public, the whole system was formally inaugurated a month later when services 26 and 46 were introduced along Ditchling Road, Preston Drove and Beaconsfield Villas.

SATURDAY 1st MAY 1976

The first London to Brighton bike ride. The low-key affair commenced from Speaker's Corner in Hyde Park with just 60 riders. The original route headed east down to and along the Old Kent Road, on to Biggin Hill and Crowborough, before splitting into two groups: a few travelled via Underhill Lane and Ditchling Beacon, the others through to Lewes and the old Lewes Road, and on to the seafront at the Palace Pier – 95 miles in total! 37 finished. The bike run, as we know it today in support of the British Heart Foundation, had its first outing in 1980 and since then more than £40 million has been raised to help fund pioneering research and patient care.

TUESDAY 2nd MAY 1815

Legendary 'dipper' Martha Gunn passed away. Born in 1726, the statuesque Brightonian became famous across the land as a bathing machine operator; she pushed the machine into, and out of, the sea and helped the bather into, and out of, the water. In over 60 years of wet ankles, Martha's skills did not go unnoticed by the Prince of Wales, who granted her free access to the royal kitchens.

MONDAY 2nd MAY 1977

Mayor, Peter Best, formally opened the lock gates between the inner and outer harbours of Brighton marina (see 24/05/1976). A jetfoil service to Dieppe commenced in April 1979, but was withdrawn in August 1980.

MONDAY 3rd MAY 1926

A general strike was called by the Trades Union Congress (TUC) to support the miners in their quarrel with the mine owners who wanted to reduce their wages by 13% and increase their shifts from seven to eight hours. Huge numbers of workers from the road transport, bus, rail, docks, printing, gas and electricity, building, iron, steel, chemicals and coal sectors stayed off work. Support in Brighton was particularly solid and the railway engineering works were stopped completely, and by the Tuesday all transport services were at a standstill. Policemen ...

A TRIO OF TROLLEYBUSES LINE UP AT THE OLD STEINE

... were ordered to sleep at their posts, and a special reserve constabulary was sworn in to deal with possible trouble. The strike in Brighton reached crisis point over the operation of the tramways with the council's tramways committee considering the use of volunteer labour to take out the trams. About 2,000 strikers marched to the Town Hall to vent their feelings but were diverted away without a deputation being received. The following day a smaller crowd of about 200 gathered in the same place. A female driver, seeing the protesters, deliberately accelerated into them and injured several people. Without stopping she drove on – with police removing strikers from the car with truncheons – and disappeared into the town.

SATURDAY 3rd MAY 1997

Quite possibly the most important and downright nerve-wracking game in the history of Brighton & Hove Albion: Hereford United away at Edgar Street, the last game of the season. Both clubs could drop out of the football league: the Bulls needed to win and the stripes needed just a point to avoid the dreaded demotion to the Conference. With no venue for home games secured for the following season, Albion fans across the world realised this could be the club's last game – ever. The 3,500-plus travelling supporters felt a sense of foreboding after 20 minutes when local lad Kerry Mayo turned a cross past his own goalkeeper Mark Ormerod. A dreadfully sombre half-time saw the players re-enter the fray to a tumultuous roar of encouragement from the away end. Striker Robbie Reinelt came on in the 55th minute. Within eight minutes, the £15,000 purchase from Colchester United made his mark. Craig Maskell controlled a poor defensive clearance on his knee before smashing a left-foot volley against the right-hand post from 20 yards. Reinelt – alert to the opportunity – won a short sprint with two defenders to drill a precise shot into the bottom corner. Cue pandemonium on the terraces! The Albion were safe! For the players, fans and officials of both clubs the game will stay in the memory for a very long time.

SATURDAY 4th MAY 1946

Performing arts promoter Harvey Goldsmith CBE was born in Middlesex. He started out as a pharmacy student at Brighton Polytechnic and began his promoting career with Club 66, a weekly student night at the Metropole. In 1985, Goldsmith organised Live Aid with Bob Geldof and has produced, managed and promoted shows with acts including; The Who, Oasis, Paul Weller, Diana Ross, Asian Dub Foundation, Supergrass, Doves, and Madness.

SATURDAY 5th MAY 1979

Over 10,000 Albion fans made the long journey to Newcastle to see if their team could join the elite of English football for the first time. Bizarrely, as Sunderland were also in the hunt for promotion, a healthy contingent of their supporters who couldn't make it to Wrexham were cheering on their bitter rivals at St James' Park! It didn't make any difference as Brian Horton's diving header from a Gary Williams cross put the visitors ahead. Peter Ward made it two and Gerry Ryan claimed a third before half-time. The First Division was just 45 minutes away! Manager Alan Mullery was clearly over-excited as he tore his players off a strip during the interval but they held on – despite the Magpies pulling one back – to claim their well-deserved place in the top tier of English football.

THURSDAY 6th MAY 2010

The people of Brighton Pavilion voted in UK's first Green MP. Caroline Lucas polled 1,250 votes more than Labour and said of the historic victory; "After the recession, after people's faith in politics has been trampled into the mud after the expenses scandal, it was not the best time to ask people to take a risk and put their faith in politics, but that is what the people of Brighton Pavilion have done." Caroline was born in Malvern, Worcestershire, in 1960, to Conservative-voting parents, attended Malvern Girls' College before graduating from the University of Exeter with a first-class BA (Hons) in English Literature. She was active in the early 1980s' peace camps at Greenham Common and Molesworth, where NATO decided to house 64 cruise missiles. Unlike Greenham – famously occupied by women only – Molesworth was also home to male protestors. One aim of the occupation was to goad the Conservative government by claiming the fence could be dismantled faster at night than it could be erected by day, and provoke an overreaction by the Ministry of Defence, gaining publicity for the anti-nuclear cause. A member of CND, the Campaign for Nuclear Disarmament, she was heavily involved in the Snowball Campaign against US military bases in the UK.

FRIDAY 7th MAY 1937

Magnus Volk made his last public appearance when a new station was opened at Black Rock. The Corporation had also built a swimming pool here and shortened the line a little. The great innovator passed away just 13 days later.

SATURDAY 8th MAY 1824

Dr James Carr, Bishop of Chichester, laid the foundation stone for Brighton's parish church, St Peter's. Standing on an island site between York Place and Richmond Place, an area once known as Richmond Green, the construction necessitated the diversion of the Lewes and Ditchling Roads.

THURSDAY 8th MAY 1913

Famous for his trademark dirty laugh, actor Sid James was born in South Africa. He worked as a diamond cutter, hairdresser, dance tutor and reputedly a part-time boxer in fairgrounds, before becoming a professional actor and moving to the UK in 1946. Sid appeared in 19 *Carry On* films, two of which were filmed in Brighton. *Carry On At Your Convenience* (1971) was the 22nd film and was the first box office failure of the series. The failure has been attributed to the attempt at exploring the political themes of the trade union movement and, crucially, portraying the union activists as buffoons – thus alienating the traditional working-class audience. The picture centres on toilet equipment manufacturers W C Boggs & Son where the traditionalist owner is having trouble. Union rep Vic Spanner continually stirs up trouble in the works, to the irritation of his co-workers and management. He calls a strike for almost any minor incident – or because he wants time off to attend a football match. A works coach trip to Brighton results in bonding between workers and management, thanks largely to that greatest of all social lubricants, alcohol. Two years later *Carry On Girls* hit the nation's cinemas where the dire seaside resort of Fircombe (Brighton) proposes a beauty contest to boost tourism. The incompetent mayor agrees to the idea but the scheme faces fierce opposition from an elegant women's liberationist. The cat fighting beauty queens take over a hotel and the competition is sabotaged. The beauty contest is supposedly held in the theatre on the West Pier and the film includes location footage of external parts of the decrepit structure. The external shots of the hotel are of Clarges – 115-119 Marine Parade – which was owned by actress Dora Bryan, who had previously appeared in the very first film of the series, *Carry On Sergeant*, in 1958.

SATURDAY 9th MAY 1953

Just in time for the Queen's coronation, the BBC's television service reached the town. England's first relay transmitter opened at the old radar station on Truleigh Hill, to the north of Shoreham, although some viewers were already receiving programmes via a cable relay from Devil's Dyke.

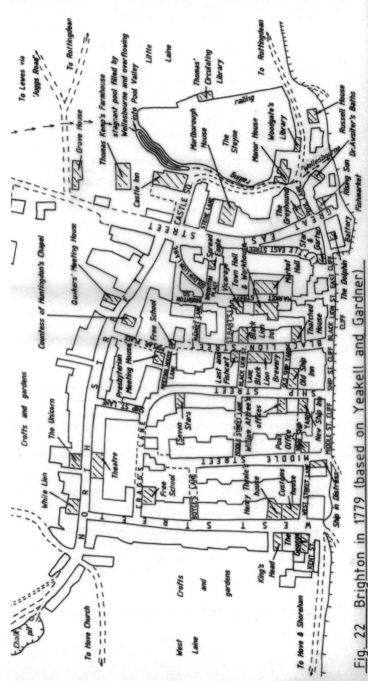

Fig. 22 Brighton in 1779 (based on Yeakell and Gardner)

SATURDAY 9th MAY 2009

Roared on by 1,000 fans from Sussex, the Brighton Blues came from behind to beat Liskeard-Looe 32-20 in the EDF Junior Vase final at Twickenham – the club's first appearance at rugby's showpiece stadium. The Cornish side held a narrow 8-7 lead at half-time, before two tries in three minutes – from player-coach Neil McGovern and Ash Hallett – helped to seal a memorable victory for the Waterhall-based side.

THURSDAY 10th MAY 1979

The Argus reported that; "Champagne could be flowing at 30,000 ft over America tomorrow night as Brighton & Hove Albion celebrate being Second Division champions." Unfortunately, Crystal Palace beat Burnley the following day in front of 51,801 Selhurst Park fans to claim the title. Both clubs were promoted to the old First Division.

MONDAY 11th MAY 1840

Brighton's first regular horse-bus service connected the Kemp Town estate to Brighton Station. By 1884 the Brighton, Hove & Preston United Omnibus Company (the 'United Company') operated 30 buses and 150 horses from stables and garages in Conway Street, Hove, now the home of Brighton & Hove buses.

TUESDAY 11th MAY 1926

The 'Battle of Lewes Road'. The General Strike dispute over the trams culminated in a fracas when 4,000 strikers gathered outside the tram depot in Lewes Road determined not to allow the trams to be driven out. Unbeknown to the gathered protesters, there was no intention of bringing the vehicles out as the volunteers were only to be trained that day. Chief Constable Charles Griffin, with 300 men on foot and 50 mounted specials, ordered the crowd to disperse. They wouldn't budge. His men advanced on foot and then brought up the specials on horseback. As the crowd was driven back to Hollingdean Road, some fighting ensued and the specials charged the crowd, lashing out with batons. As the strikers hit back a vicious struggle broke out. Eventually the crowd, in which there were many children, dissipated but two people were left seriously injured and many others were hurt. That night there was another disturbance outside the Brighton & District Labour Club at 93 London Road when another five people were arrested. The nationwide strike lasted ten days from May 3rd. It was called by the general council of the Trades Union Congress (TUC) in an unsuccessful attempt to force the British government to act to prevent wage reduction and worsening conditions for 800,000 locked-out coal miners.

SATURDAY 11th MAY 1991

A run of a solitary victory in six games meant Brighton & Hove Albion must beat Ipswich Town in Hove to stay in contention of a trip to Wembley. Mike Small fired the home side in front before Player of the Year Perry Digweed sprung into action to save a penalty from Chris Kiwomya, who would level the scores with ten minutes remaining. John Byrne was fouled just outside the box as the seconds ticked down. Dean Wilkins and Robert Codner debated who should take the direct free kick and the former usurped the latter to curl the ball into the top corner past the despairing dive of one-cap-wonder Phil Parkes (the flying hippo) to spark wild scenes on the terraces. Albion were in the play-offs!

MONDAY 12th MAY 1980

The first new station in the Southern Region (as it was then) for 12 years, Moulsecoomb Station accepted passengers for the first time.

SATURDAY 13th MAY 2000

The Argus reported that Brighton and Hove had the highest percentage of profit-making companies in the country. According to a survey, the then towns came first out of 162 contemporaries with 92.3% of large businesses in the black. The regeneration of the town centre and seafront was instrumental in the boom, along with the influx of multi-media and new technology businesses. Ken Bodfish, executive councillor for regeneration, said: "We have always been well known as a place to enjoy yourself. This survey shows that this can go hand-in-hand with a businesslike, efficient environment in which companies can flourish."

SUNDAY 14th MAY 1843

A large stock of candles – over 50,000 – was removed from the lower part of Mr Broad's candle manufactory in Spring Gardens, Brighton, as the upper portion was enveloped in flames. Locating water was a problem, as The Times explained: "...the engine was found to be useless, the water running from the engine nearly as fast as it was poured in, and the small quantity that found its way through the hose having about as much effect on the flames as a boy's squirt..." No-one perished in the fire but Mr Broad's wife and children were severely burnt in the accident. "...A large quantity of the candles removed from the store... as well as furniture from the adjoining houses, was, we regret to say, carried off by the [assembled] crowd... The same building was partially consumed by fire 13 years ago, when the mob who assembled at the spot behaved so badly that the military was called out to keep guard with their swords drawn..."

SATURDAY 14th MAY 1938

The country's first Municipal Camping and Caravan Ground, to the north of East Brighton Park in Sheepcote Valley, opened.

TUESDAY 15th MAY 1984

The Argus reported: "One more chapter of Brighton's history will come to an end on May 26th when Bolton's egg shop in Gardner Street closes. The business began 100 years ago and deliveries will continue after the shop shuts. Mr Henry Bolton began his egg business when he opened his first shop in Westbourne Gardens, Hove, in 1886." It moved to Brighton in 1910. "...The fact that fewer people had bacon and eggs for breakfast had hit sales." Henry's wife said; "After all, you can't freeze eggs."

SATURDAY 15th MAY 2010

The Brighton Blues won their second Twickenham final in two years. Achieving the same points tally as last year's game, the Sussex side smashed Coventry's Dunlop 32-3 to lift the Senior Vase, having taken the Junior Vase 12 months earlier. An Ed Court try gave the Blues a 5-3 lead at half-time before the sin-binning of Dunlop flanker Gerrard Clough, early in the second half, proved the turning point as Brighton ran in two quick tries through centre Ed Court and lock Mark Gibb. Blues player-coach Neil McGovern told BBC Sussex: "It's been an incredible two years at the club. It's down to the boys and the effort and attitude they've shown. Hopefully, we can keep the side together and push on as a club."

TUESDAY 16th MAY 1961

Brighton's town-centre slums have been sporadically cleared over the centuries. One such initiative in the early 1960s – Highleigh, one of four blocks of flats built in phase one of the Albion Hill redevelopment – was officially opened by the mayor, Alan Johnson. The area, to the east of St Peter's Church, is afforded excellent views of the town.

SUNDAY 17th MAY 1964

This Whitsun weekend saw the invasion of two rival youth cultures – the Mods and Rockers – who ran riot along Brighton seafront. The BBC report read; "...In Brighton, two youths were jailed for three months and others were fined. More than 1,000 teenagers were involved in skirmishes on the beach and the promenade last night. They threw deckchairs around, broke them up to make bonfires, shouted

Brighton & Hove On This Day

obscenities at each other and at passers-by, jostled holidaymakers and
terrified elderly residents. At about 1300 BST Mods and Rockers
gathered at the Palace Pier chanting and jeering at each other and threw
stones when police tried to disperse them. The teenagers staged a mass
sit-down on the promenade when police, using horses and dogs, tried
to move them on."

TUESDAY 17th MAY 1966

Police reinforcements were called to the Goldstone Ground to stop
youths behind the goal throwing orange-peel and whistling during a
reserve game against Notts County.

SATURDAY 17th MAY 1980

The Red Arrows RAF display team suffered a major blip as Squadron
Leader Stephen Johnson's Hawk clipped a yacht's mast and plunged
into the sea. The pilot escaped and the incident led to the change in
permitted minimum flying height from 35 feet to 100 feet.

FRIDAY 18th MAY 1900

On the second day of a three-day game, Kumar Shri Ranjitsinhji notched
36 runs against Worcestershire at the County Ground, Hove. Born in
India in 1872, 'Ranji' is widely regarded as one of the greatest batsmen
of all time and arrived at Sussex in 1893. He represented England for
the first time in 1896 and became the first batsman to score hundreds
on his debut home and away Tests. The feat was eventually emulated by
Andrew Strauss 108 years later.

THURSDAY 19th MAY 2011

A Glasgow man won more than £300,000 on a £1 horse bet, including
races at Brighton. "I regularly place these little bets and everyone tells
me I'm mad." A spokesman for William Hill said: "He's our luckiest
ever punter."

SATURDAY 20th MAY 1899

The Brighton Marine Palace & Pier Company proudly opened their
masterpiece – the Palace Pier. On condition of the Chain Pier's removal,
the first screw-pile of the new structure was driven in in November 1891.
A storm destroyed the Chain Pier in December 1896 – thus avoiding the
necessity of demolition – but the wreckage damaged not only the new
adjacent structure but also both the West Pier and Volk's Railway, the
resultant damages claims threatening the new venture. The pier was ...

... extended slightly in 1938 when a 'big wheel' was added at the head, but it was closed throughout the war – when it was damaged by German bombs – and a gap was made near the middle to prevent its possible use as a landing stage. The theatre was removed in 1986 and in 2000 signs proclaiming 'Brighton Pier' replaced the Palace Pier insignia. The alteration is not recognised by the National Piers Society, many Brighton and Hove residents, and *The Argus*. The pier is listed at Grade II and, as of February 2001, was one of 70 Grade II*-listed buildings and structures, and 1,218 listed buildings of all grades, in the city.

SATURDAY 21st MAY 1983

An unforgettable day. Brighton & Hove Albion faced Manchester United in the FA Cup Final at Wembley in front of 100,000 fans, and many millions more worldwide on TV. The team flew into north London courtesy of a British Caledonian (the club's sponsors) helicopter. Tony Grealish led the team out, sporting a white headband in sympathy for the suspended Steve Foster. On 13 minutes, Gary Howlett floated a cross into the box for Gordon Smith to head into the bottom of the net – 1-0 Albion in the cup final! In the second half, Chris Ramsey was injured by Norman Whiteside and forced off, but not before Frank Stapleton had equalised with Ramsey limping behind him. Ray Wilkins then curled a delightful shot around Graham Moseley but hadn't reckoned on Gary Stevens. The Man of the Match equalised four minutes from the final whistle, firing in from a short corner. In the very last minute of extra time Michael Robinson shrugged off Kevin Moran and passed across the box to Gordon Smith. Commentator Peter Jones famously screamed, "and Smith must score" as goalkeeper Gary Bailey saved the Scotsman's low shot with his legs. The final whistle blew 21 seconds later! At the club's 25th anniversary of the cup final meal at the Grand Hotel, the Scot intimated that he should have 'whacked it' instead of placing his effort.

THURSDAY 22nd MAY 1947

Used during World War II as a mortuary, Withdean Stadium was re-launched as the Brighton Olympic Stadium. It flopped and closed five years later. At this juncture, Brighton Council decided to convert the venue into an athletics arena and on May 14th 1955 the mayor, Walter Dudeney, formally opened the venue. The original Withdean Stadium began life in 1936 as the finest tennis centre outside Wimbledon and was set to host the South of England Championships until the war intervened. The Davis Cup match between Great Britain and New Zealand was held there in the spring of 1939.

SATURDAY 23rd MAY 1992

Brighton's first 'official' Gay Pride march took place. Hundreds of people gathered at the Peace statue for an afternoon of festivities. The parade was part of an 11-day gay festival, the largest to be staged in the UK.

MONDAY 24th MAY 1686

The earliest known record of local post boys – who were controlled by the General Post Office – was an advertisement in the *London Gazette* on this day which announced that post boys on pack horses left for Brighthelmston, and other places, on Monday nights, returning the next day. Postage was paid by the recipients. Some of the boys were only 11 or 12.

MONDAY 24th MAY 1773

Following the incorporation of the Brighton Town Act, the first meeting was held at the Castle Inn. The Act empowered the commissioners to levy a rate of up to three shillings in the pound for the purposes of lighting, paving and cleansing the streets. An interesting clause required inhabitants to sweep the pavements outside their houses between 8am and 10am every day, except Sunday. The 'sport' of cock-throwing, the slaughtering of animals in streets, and public bonfires and fireworks, were all banned.

SUNDAY 24th MAY 1908

The beautiful St Anne's Well Gardens in Hove was opened as a public park. Dr Richard Russell developed the park's spring as a small spa, erecting a basin circa 1750. A pump room catered for the fashionable visitor around 1830 but its popularity waned and the area became a private pleasure garden 20 years later.

MONDAY 24th MAY 1976

Long before bits of the cliff fell onto Asda below, the last of the 110 concrete caissons were dropped into the sea at Black Rock. The 38-feet high concrete-filled structures – 40 feet in diameter and weighing 600 tons – formed the outer wall of Brighton Marina. The inner wall was finished in June 1975 to complete the 77 acres of sheltered water. Schemes for harbours had been proposed since at least the early 19th century but only one came to fruition. Garage proprietor Henry Cohen, whose group commissioned a plan from architects Overton and Partners which was put to the council, conceived the idea in October 1963. The ambitious original development – including 3,000 yacht berths, helicopter and hovercraft stations, conference hall, hotel, shops, ...

... flats, restaurant, clubs, swimming pool, casino, bowling alley, cinemas, theatre and car parks – was to be sited to the west of Duke's Mound. The residents of Kemp Town opposed the plan. In September 1965, a revised £11 million plan was approved provided no building projected above the cliffs. The gyratory access road system – which involved the demolition of Rifle Butt Road and other houses of Black Rock – was eventually passed through Parliament as the Brighton Corporation Act in July 1970.

SATURDAY 25th MAY 1822

The *Swift* made its maiden journey. Once the busiest cross-Channel port in England, Brighton was the quickest route between London and Paris as overland speeds were roughly the same as those at sea. In 1764, a regular packet service commenced between Brighton and Dieppe, but following the end of the Napoleonic Wars there was an increase in traffic in 1817 with nearly 2,500 passengers travelling to France during that summer. The *Swift* was the first of many steam ships on the route.

MONDAY 25th MAY 1846

To celebrate the Queen's 27th birthday, the 32-feet high Victoria Fountain was inaugurated towards the south end of the Old Steine. To commemorate the event, local musician Charles Coote composed the Fountain Quadrilles.

THURSDAY 26th MAY 1983

The FA Cup Final replay was contested at Wembley Stadium. Led by the returning Steve Foster, Brighton & Hove Albion narrowly lost 4-0 to Manchester United.

SATURDAY 27th MAY 2006

Day nine in the *Big Brother* house. Brightonian Pete Bennett went on to win the seventh – and most popular in the show's ten-year history – series of the Channel 4 television programme where they seclude a group of deluded idiots away from outside influences for the nation's 'entertainment'.

TUESDAY 28th MAY 2002

The Argus reported on the arrival of Jordan's first child, Harvey. The model, real name Katie Price, was born in Brighton in 1978 and has gone on to make millions from books, reality TV, marrying Peter Andre and exposing her (fake) breasts.

TUESDAY 29th MAY 1660

Pinch-Bum Day. Oak Apple Day, to use its proper term, is steeped in tradition and, far from being sordid, it was once a public holiday. According to famous diarist Samuel Pepys; "Parliament had ordered the 29 of May, the King's [Charles II] birthday, to be for ever kept as a day of thanksgiving for our redemption from tyranny and the King's return to his Government, he entering London that day." The event symbolised Charles II hiding in a tree after the Battle of Worcester, which enabled his eventual accession to the throne, and remained for around 200 years, being marked by the wearing of oak apples and sprigs. In some parts of the country the celebration, particularly in Brighton, became known as Pinch-Bum Day because those not wearing an oak sprig (a sign of loyalty to the restored King) were liable to be set upon under threat of having their bottoms pinched.

TUESDAY 29th MAY 1855

The 1855 Brighton Commissioners Transfer Act dissolved the town commissioners and vested all their powers, privileges, liabilities and property – including the Royal Pavilion, the market and the Town Hall – into the new corporation. The last meeting was held the day before.

TUESDAY 30th MAY 1854

The new Borough of Brighton's first elections were held. The earliest known attempt to incorporate the town as a borough was in 1684 when Charles II apparently favoured a petition – it was not heard of again. By the start of the 19th century the town had grown sufficiently for incorporation to be suggested, but the idea was rejected at a town meeting in July 1806 due to the probable expense. The 'Great Reform Act' of 1832 created the Parliamentary Borough of Brighton, but municipal government continued from the town commissioners and the vestry and in April 1848 a town poll again rejected incorporation, but petitions for and against were sent to the Privy Council in 1852 which, after an eleven-day public inquiry, found in favour of the 'non-incorporationists'. Another petition and Privy Council inquiry in August 1853 was successful and resulted in the award of a charter of incorporation on January 19th 1854.

SUNDAY 30th MAY 2004

Albion headed to Cardiff to face Bristol City in the Second Division Play-Off Final. Manager Mark McGhee sent out the unused substitutes to warm-up with instructions to gee up the fans. Just a few moments ...

... later – in the 84th minute – striker Chris Iwelumo played a one-two with Leon Knight and was fouled. The pint-sized striker converted the penalty to send the 31,000 Seagulls fans into raptures. Albion were in the Championship!

MONDAY 31st MAY 1937

The inaugural flight from Shoreham Airport to Jersey – in a four-engined De Havilland biplane – operated by Jersey Airways, flew the 150 miles in 75 minutes.

THURSDAY 31st MAY 1973

The facade of the St Dunstan's Institute, a listed building and recently restored and extended, reopened. St Dunstan's was originally established in 1915 at the Bayswater Road, London by Sir Arthur Pearson – a newspaper proprietor who owned the *Evening Standard*, and founded the *Daily Express*, who lost his own sight through glaucoma – for men and women blinded on war service. The Ovingdean convalescent home was constructed between 1937 and 1939. The seven-storey orange-brick building has twice been visited by Queen Elizabeth II and Prince Philip and is now used for training, holidays and convalescence.

FRIDAY 31st MAY 1974

The number of empty properties in Brighton angered locals, and the many homeless people who began to squat. 'The siege of Terminus Road' came to a head today as the derelict council house occupied by 27-year-old artist Pat Flynn, his wife and four children, was ordered to be vacated by a judge. The bailiffs arrived to evict them as demonstrators, armed with a megaphone, flour, sand, and coffee, scuffled with police. Young teacher, David Bell, chained himself to the front door and after three attempts was eventually freed.

THURSDAY 31st MAY 1979

Her Majesty Queen Elizabeth II toured the Lanes. Forming the heart of the Old Town, the world famous area was partially developed during the late 16th and early 17th centuries as the population of the small fishing town grew. Established between 1120 and 1147, the small chapel and priory of St Bartholomew once stood on the site of Bartholomew House. Partially destroyed by French raiders in 1514, the priory was dissolved 33 years later under Henry VIII. Just up the road is the oldest town centre pub in Brighton, the Cricketers Arms – a listed building – that probably dates from the 17th century when it was known as the

'Last (a measure of 10,000 herrings) and Fishcart'. A few hundred yards west Boyce's Street – linking Middle Street and West Street – was home of the Sussex & Brighton Infirmary for Diseases of the Eye from 1832 until 1846. Back towards the Steine – and the eastern edge of the Lanes – is the relatively recent development of Brighton Square, ahead of its time when it was built in 1966, but a bit dated now. Bounded by North Street to the north, Ship Street to the west and Prince Albert Street and the north side of Bartholomew Square to the south, the eastern boundary is less well-defined and can be considered either East Street or Market Street. Until the 1930s, the Lanes were considered shabby and unworthy of Brighton and if Sir Herbert Carden had had his way, the area could have become Croydon-by-the-Sea. Later on this very day Her Majesty officially opened Brighton Marina.

JUNE

MONDAY 1st JUNE 1981

Zimbabwe's Home Affairs Minister, Richard Hove, said his government had declared war on the country's bandits. More police were to be deployed with the recent crime wave in the year-old country. The former Cabinet Minister; Politburo Secretary for Economic Affairs and Planning Commissioner died in 2009.

SATURDAY 2nd JUNE 1928

Just two years after the first greyhound meeting in the country, Hove's greyhound stadium opened on Nevill Road, near the Goldstone Ground. The original arena was furnished with redundant fittings and materials from the old Brighton Aquarium and has hosted athletics, football, horse shows, military tattoos, boxing matches, American football and rugby.

SATURDAY 2nd JUNE 1962

The country's first casino opened at the Metropole Hotel on Brighton seafront, in the Clarence Room. The casino's walk-in safe can still be seen and is impossible to remove without demolishing part of the building. The casino moved to the International Casino in Preston Street in 1985.

SUNDAY 2nd JUNE 1991

Around 32,400 Brighton & Hove Albion fans – out of a 59,940 total – followed the club to the twin towers, the biggest away following in the Albion's history, for the Second Division Play-Off Final. Wearing the infamous red 'Chewits wrapper' kit, the club's third Wembley visit ended in a 3-1 defeat to Notts County. Supporters were unaware of the hideous shirts and shorts combo – which both had the same shocking pink pattern – before the game commenced. Dean Wilkins netted the consolation just before the final whistle.

MONDAY 2nd JUNE 1997

The bulldozers moved in to begin the demolition of the 96-year-old Goldstone Football Ground. A truly sad day for football in Brighton, Hove, Sussex and beyond.

THURSDAY 3rd JUNE 2010

An outbreak of mumps was sweeping across Brighton and Hove with 46 confirmed cases of the virus since January, compared to 27 for the whole of 2009.

FRIDAY 4th JUNE 1999

For once, Herbert Whitfield was glad to see a bit of summer rain – the septuagenarian had been trapped in his bath for three days! He was saved when neighbour John Broadfoot went into his garden for a deserved beer after a hard day at work. It started to rain so John headed in and noticed a mumbling sound emanating from his friend Herbert's bathroom in Morecambe Road, Brighton. John said; "If it had been raining I would definitely not have gone out. Another day and things could have been a lot worse. This has taught me how important it is to keep an eye out for your neighbours." Mr Whitfield was said to be in a stable condition.

TUESDAY 5th JUNE 2007

Extra police officers patrolled the streets of Brighton because there was a full moon! It followed research by the force which concluded there was a rise in violent incidents at these times – and also on paydays! Inspector Andy Parr commented; "From my experience, over 19 years of being a police officer, undoubtedly on full moons, we do seem to get people with, sort of, stranger behaviour – more fractious, argumentative."

THURSDAY 6th JUNE 1872

Sussex's first county cricket match was played at Eaton Road against Gloucestershire.

WEDNESDAY 7th JUNE 1854

Brighton's first mayor, Lieutenant-Colonel John Fawcett, was elected at the first council meeting.

MONDAY 7th JUNE 1971

The British Engineerium in Hove was listed by the Historic Buildings Council for England (the predecessor of English Heritage) after it was threatened with demolition. The facility had supplied water to the local area for more than a century before it was converted. In 1858, the Victorian engineer Thomas Hawksley declared that the chalk basin of the Goldstone Valley was the perfect place to extract a lasting water supply for Brighton and Hove. The Goldstone Pumping Station was opened by the Brighton and Hove Constant Water Company in 1866. The water was drawn by an Eastern & Amos 120 hp beam engine from the 160 ft Goldstone Bottom well and it could raise 130,000 gallons an hour. Header tunnels – extending for 1,800 feet to help collect water as it runs through the chalk – were dug out, roughly in parallel ...

... with the sea. In 1872 the water supply was increased with the addition of a No. 2 Engine which can produce 150,000 gallons an hour and was in daily service until 1952 when steam power was finally replaced. By the 1970s, the pumping station and its machines were on the verge of demolition until a group of enthusiasts came to the rescue in 1974. The British Engineerium opened two years later.

SUNDAY 8th JUNE 1930

Beatrice Prendergast was stabbed to death in an alley off St James' Street, Brighton. She had three knife wounds and was clutching two half-crowns in her right hand when her body was found by Mr J W Nye, whose car headlights picked out the 56-year-old. The lady had been living in Cavendish Street, a slum area, and the post mortem revealed that two wounds had pierced the heart, while the third broke a rib.

FRIDAY 9th JUNE 1911

Leading 20th century dramatist Sir Terence Mervyn Rattigan was born. Among his many works are the screenplays for *Brighton Rock* (1947) and *Goodbye, Mr Chips* (1969).

MONDAY 10th JUNE 1839

Sussex County Cricket Club played their inaugural first-class match versus Marylebone Cricket Club at Lord's.

MONDAY 11th JUNE 2007

The Brighton-based band Blood Red Shoes released the single, *It's Getting Boring By The Sea*, on V2 Records. Early in their careers, the alternative rock duo were prolific in releasing limited edition 7" vinyl pressings.

THURSDAY 12th JUNE 1947

Actor Laurence Olivier was created Knight Bachelor – the most basic rank of a man who has been knighted by the monarch but not as a member of one of the organised Orders of Chivalry – on this day. Born in 1907, he is famous for his lead roles and in June 1970 was created a life peer in the Queen's Birthday Honours as Baron Olivier, of Brighton, the first actor to be afforded this distinction.

WEDNESDAY 13th JUNE 1973

Brighton & Hove Albion lost one of its favourite sons; Charlie Webb passed away in Hove aged 86. Such was the inside-left's love of the club that he turned down a chance to manage Tottenham Hotspur before World War II.

SUNDAY 13th JUNE 2010

Thousands of people stripped naked, adorned their bodies in tassels, loincloths, swimming trunks – and a cheeky smile – to take part in the fifth World Naked Bike Ride through the streets of Brighton and Hove.

SATURDAY 14th JUNE 2003

The Isetta Owners Club of Great Britain presented a plaque to the Brighton Station car park site commemorating 50 years of the bubble car. The Isetta was a small one-door car, designed in Italy by a company called Iso. In March 1957 the Southern Locomotive works on New England Street finished its last railway job and, six weeks later, re-opened to assemble Isettas, employing 200 locals. All the parts had to be brought in by railway, as the factory had no road access. The factory made its last vehicle in 1964.

MONDAY 15th JUNE 2009

Brighton Magistrates' Court heard how a Whitehawk man was guilty of allowing his five-year-old border collie to become twice its ideal weight. A 63-year-old man was disqualified from keeping any other animals for 12 months.

SATURDAY 16th JUNE 2007

June 16th is the saint day of St Richard, patron saint of Sussex. Sussex Day was dreamed up by West Sussex County Council as an opportunity to; "Celebrate the rich heritage of the county." The Sussex motto is 'We Won't Be Druv' ('no-one can tell us what to do') and the county was the last in England to be converted to Christianity.

SUNDAY 17th JUNE 1934

The torso of a woman was discovered when a particularly fragrant unclaimed plywood trunk was noticed by William Joseph Vinnicombe at the left luggage office of Brighton railway station. The following day a similar trunk containing what proved to be the limbs of the same body was discovered at King's Cross railway station, London. In the course of police investigations, Jack Notyre – alias Toni Mancini, and alias Cecil Louis England – a waiter at the Skylake Café in Brighton, was interviewed concerning the disappearance of his cohabiter ...

... Violet Kaye, a 42-year-old dancer and prostitute affected by drink and drugs. Kaye and Mancini's relationship was tempestuous and one argument at Mancini's workplace saw an obviously drunk Kaye accusing him of being familiar with a teenage waitress. She was never seen again. Mancini told friends she had gone to Paris, and gave some of her clothes and belongings to the waitress. Violet's body was in a large trunk at the bottom of his bed, covered with a cloth and used as a coffee table – in spite of the smell and the fluids that had began to leak. Mancini was tried for Kaye's murder at Lewes Assizes and acquitted. The Courts of Assize, or Assizes, were periodic criminal courts held around England and Wales until 1972. They were abolished by the Courts Act 1971 and replaced by a single permanent Crown Court. The victim of the first murder remained unidentified and the crime unsolved.

WEDNESDAY 18th JUNE 2003

The Argus explained how a mini-stadium, fit for international beach football, could be built on Brighton beach. Organisers of the previous year's tournament said a permanent venue could have 4,000 seats, corporate facilities and be used for other events such as horse shows, concerts, netball and basketball events. The previous year, more than 9,000 spectators watched as big names such as Eric Cantona, Matt Le Tissier and Bob Booker battled it out on the sand.

FRIDAY 19th JUNE 1931

The founder of Brighton & Hove Albion Football Club, John Jackson, died at the age of 70. The son of a Birmingham master toolmaker, John represented Coventry Rangers between the sticks before coaching at Liverpool and Leicester Fosse before arriving on the coast in 1901.

FRIDAY 20th JUNE 1856

Sussex CCC entertained Surrey at the Royal Brunswick Ground in Hove. The three-day game ended in victory for the opposition.

MONDAY 21st JUNE 2004

Iconic 1960s Mod brand Ben Sherman was sold to US clothing manufacturer Oxford Industries in an £80 million deal. The company founder, Arthur Bernard Sugarman, was born in Brighton in 1925 and launched his line of button-down shirts in 1963, just in time for the burgeoning Mod movement. He opened a store on London's Carnaby Street a year later before his first Brighton outlet in Duke's Street welcomed customers in 1967.

SEVEN STARS
YOUNGS
YOUNGS

TUESDAY 22nd JUNE 1999

Grand Hotel bomber Patrick Magee was released from the Maze Prison in Belfast. The IRA man was given eight life sentences for the atrocity. Prime Minister Tony Blair admitted the situation was "very hard to stomach". Amazingly, since leaving the Maze, Magee has formed an organisation promoting peace and conflict resolution – buildingbridgesforpeace.org – with Jo Berry, the daughter of one of his victims, Sir Anthony Berry MP.

FRIDAY 23rd JUNE 2000

The floral clock in Palmeira Square was vandalised. Installed by the old Hove Council to mark the Queen's Coronation in 1953, the timepiece's hands were damaged, along with the mechanism.

MONDAY 24th JUNE 1867

Famous for staging the Eurovision Song Contest (see 06/04/1974) when ABBA were victorious with *Waterloo*, The Dome opened its doors for the first time. Following the purchase of the Royal Pavilion estate in 1850, the stables and riding house were used as cavalry barracks from 1856, until about 1864, before the interior was reconstructed as a concert hall – at a cost of £10,000 – to a Moorish design. The original building housed 2,500 people and was fitted with a beautiful gas chandelier 30 feet high, and 16 feet in diameter, with 1,300 gas jets.

MONDAY 24th JUNE 1901

Brighton & Hove Albion Football Club came into being on this very day at the Seven Stars Public House in Ship Street, Brighton. John Jackson – who had previously been involved with the town's other two outfits, United and Rangers – was hoping for third time lucky this time around. The new club was to be christened Brighton & Hove United but Hove Football Club objected on the grounds that they would lose support as the public may assume United were a merger of the former United and Rangers. As a result the Albion was born. The origins of the name are unclear but two reasons stand out: the town had many businesses with the Albion suffix, or it was because founder John Jackson had close links with West Bromwich Albion.

TUESDAY 25th JUNE 1985

All 140 members of the Brighton & Hove Hotels and Guesthouse Association were put on red alert as Scotland Yard announced that the IRA had planned a bombing campaign in at least 12 towns across the UK.

SATURDAY 26th JUNE 1830

The Prince Regent, George IV, or King George, has left a lasting legacy to the place he called home for a significant portion of his extraordinary life. When he turned 21, in 1783, he obtained a grant of £60,000 (equal to £5,744,000 today) from Parliament and an annual income of £50,000 (£4,786,000 today) from his father, George III. His charm and culture earned him the title 'the first gentleman of England', but his frivolous ways earned him the contempt of the people. In 1811, he became regent after his father was declared insane and he was able to indulge his love for parades and spectacle after the final defeat of Napoleon by Britain and her allies in 1815. George's dream of a fantastical seaside palace and spa became a reality when John Nash's Royal Pavilion was completed in 1822. Throughout his adult life, George was an important artistic patron, acquiring an impressive collection of art and patronising architects and designers, most notably at Brighton. In his later years George had little involvement in government and spent his time in seclusion at Windsor Castle. His only child, Princess Charlotte, had died in childbirth in 1817 so the crown passed to George's brother who became William IV.

SATURDAY 27th JUNE 1807

The Theatre Royal first opened its doors to the public with a performance of *Hamlet* and *The Weather Cock* starring Charles Kemble. The Grade II listed building is one of the oldest working theatres in the country and for the first 50 years suffered very mixed fortunes with no single manager lasting more than 18 months – and the risk of financial ruin never very far away. Actor Henry John Nye Chart took over management in 1854 and turned its fortunes and reputation around. By the end of the 19th century the Theatre Royal had established itself as 'the actors' theatre' where every major thespian including the Kemble and Siddon families, Sarah Bernhardt, Edmund Kean, David Garrick and Sir Henry Irving graced the stage. In 1894, a safety curtain and additional exits were installed, the backstage area was improved with a new stage door and the dressing rooms were revamped following the purchase of 35-38 Bond Street. The most significant developments came from the integration into the main theatre of 9 New Road, the former home of the Nye Charts (Mrs Nye Chart having donated her house to the theatre upon her death two years previously). This allowed for the creation of a new main entrance and the re-location of the box office using what had been the Nye Charts' ground floor, hence the presence of the domestic fireplace, still in evidence today. The period immediately following World War I saw the acquisition of a number of adjacent properties including, in 1923, the Colonnade Hotel, now known as the ...

... Colonnade Bar. No lasting changes were made almost until the end of the century when the theatre was substantially refurbished. Today, the building's long and uninterrupted history is clear through the reclaimed timber frames to the original gaslight fittings, the boarded-up window leading nowhere in the Royal Circle to the domestic fireplace in the main foyer: evidence of the theatre's organic growth over two centuries.

SATURDAY 28th JUNE 1810

Horses, carts and people used the Bolney to Pyecombe section of the old A23 London-Brighton road for the first time. As it leaves the borough of Brighton and Hove, the road runs the length of the former parish of Patcham from the Preston boundary near Clermont Road, through Withdean and Patcham village to the Pylons and beyond. In 1770 it became the Cuckfield 'Turnpike' and tollgates were situated at South Road, in Preston Village, and Mill Road.

SUNDAY 28th JUNE 1970

One of the best players in Sussex County Cricket Club's history, Mushtaq Ahmed, was born in Sahiwal, Pakistan. The 5ft 4ins. spin bowler was famous for his hard-to-pick googly and joined Sussex in 2003, helping the county to their first-ever county championship in his first season. He played his part in the title successes of 2006 and 2007 with 102 and 90-wicket hauls.

FRIDAY 29th JUNE 1934

Thirty-one years before it was torn down in order to make way for the hideous concrete carbuncle that was Churchill Square (version one), the Brighton Sports Stadium (SS Brighton) welcomed punters for the first time. Billed as the 'largest covered seawater swimming pool in the world', one of the first people to dive from the ten-metre diving platform was Johnny Weissmuller, Olympic world champion, who would find Hollywood fame as Tarzan. The summers of 1934 and 1935 were sweltering and Brightonians preferred their seawater swimming in its usual surroundings – just a few yards down the road. Ironically, due to the hot weather, the management decided to turn the pool into an ice rink – the pool lasted just 15 months – and the first customers skated through the doors three months later. The new rink – still known as the SS Brighton – was an instant success and the top entertainment venue on the south coast for the next three decades. On the same day, the first Brighton Belle train ran on the Brighton to London Victoria line. The luxurious mode of transport operated until April 1972, when it was taken out of service. The original carriages were restored and re-instated on the route and chugged out of Brighton station in time for the 2012 Olympics in London.

FRIDAY 30th JUNE 2006

The Argus reported that the war medals of former Albion chairman Captain William Charles 'Carlo' Campbell were to be auctioned. He was decorated for gallantry while flying more than 20 sorties within a few months during World War I but was best known for an abortive bid to bring cheetah racing to Britain in 1937. He imported six cheetahs to perk up greyhound racing at the White City track in west London but the 70 mph creatures failed to muster the necessary competitive spirit. An observer recalled that, "they just wandered about".

JULY

TUESDAY 1st JULY 2008

The Argus reported on the proposed route for the Brighton and Hove monorail. "The futuristic transport system is planned to link Brighton Marina to Shoreham harbour under a multimillion-pound scheme. The trains would connect the marina, Palace Pier, Brighton Centre, King Alfred, Shoreham harbour and Shoreham airport."

TUESDAY 2nd JULY 1935

The four-storey Sussex Eye Hospital in Eastern Road opened. Founded in 1832 at 2 Boyces Street as the Sussex and Brighton Infirmary for Diseases of the Eye, in November 1846 a new building was opened at 104 Queen's Road, which became the premises of the Royal National Institute for the Blind and the Moon Society's publishing works. It was demolished in 1961 and replaced by Equity and Law House.

SATURDAY 3rd JULY 1920

The climax of 'Hove Baby Week' was a pram parade from Clarendon Villas Hall to St Ann's Well Gardens for the presentation of the prizes won at the Baby Show.

FRIDAY 3rd JULY 1959

Headline in *The Times*: YOUTH OF BRIGHTON 'BORED'. "After a seven-month inquiry a team of 12 businessmen, clergymen, and professional people last night issued their views on the youth of Brighton... the picture is one of a bored younger generation with a tendency to drift, but the investigators – a commission set up by Brighton Education Committee – found that the Teddy Boy problem as it possibly exists in other areas is not outstanding in Brighton. The commission's report speaks of the attraction of coffee bars (with their juke box), which take the form of meeting places and social clubs. One coffee bar had 1,000 members... The Committee suggest that new multi-storey flats are built and basements should be for used by youth organisations."

TUESDAY 4th JULY 1865

Nowadays there seems to be a hundred and one pointless 'gossip' and 'fashion' magazines that compete for the latest celebrity non-entity tittle tattle. It wasn't always like this. The fantastically titled *Brighton Fashionable Visitors List* was first published on this day and came out every Tuesday, Thursday and Saturday. In order to – one would assume – appeal to a wider audience the publication changed its name slightly to

Brighton Standard & Fashionable Visitors List 13 years later. On March 4th 1953, after a total of 13,249 editions, the *BSAFV* ceased to be.

TUESDAY 4th JULY 1911

Shoreham Airport was the starting point for the first recorded cargo flight when Horatio Barber, in his Valkyrie monoplane, flew a box of Osram light bulbs to nearby Hove. Just over 18 months earlier, London-based artist Harold Piffard had set himself up on a piece of grazing land across the river from Shoreham, and by the end of 1910 others had arrived and the flying ground was established. The period leading up to World War I saw many companies and individuals establishing buildings on the south side of the site. With the war over, the fledgling Canadian Air force moved in and spent time training and testing some of the 65 captured German aircraft that were stored at the airfield. By December 1921, all activity on the airfield stopped and for the next few years it reverted to grazing land. In 1930 the municipal authorities of Brighton, Hove and Worthing formed a joint committee to establish Shoreham as the municipal airport for the three towns and construction on the terminal building – now a Grade II listed building – began in November 1934. The German invasion of France in 1940 caused passenger traffic to cease and after a short break the Royal Air Force took over the airport. With fighter airfields already established close by it was decided to base part of the newly formed 277 Air Sea Rescue Squadron at Shoreham. Equipped with Spitfires, Walrus amphibians, Deviants and Lysanders the squadron was involved in the rescue of nearly 600 airmen from the English Channel. In 1971, Shoreham became a municipal airport again under the control of the three local councils; passenger services and general aviation became the focus of attention.

TUESDAY 4th JULY 1933

Minister of Health Sir Hilton Young formally opened the Undercliff Walk – from Black Rock to Rottingdean, about 2.3 miles – at Ovingdean Gap. Over three years, the construction cost £360,000, used 13,000 tons of cement, 150,000 concrete blocks, and 500 men at a time of severe depression, although there was controversy over the 'importation' of Welsh miners to do skilled rock work. The extension to Saltdean Gap was formally opened by the mayor, Edward Denne, some three weeks later. Great damage to the Walk was caused by the storms of February 1990, causing certain sections to be closed off, resulting in a £7 million repair scheme. The cliff exposures make this an important collecting site for faunas of the upper Santonian and lower Campanian ages (700,000 years ago).

FRIDAY 5th JULY 1771

Dr Richard Russell, who advocated the health benefits of drinking seawater, thus precipitating the village's ascent into a thriving town, died on this day, although the *Gentleman's Magazine* believed he died in 1759. In 1750, Russell published a Latin dissertation De Tabe Glandulari, where he recommended the use of seawater – particularly around Brighton – for the cure of enlarged lymphatic glands. After his passing, his Old Steine house was rented to seasonal visitors, including the brother of George III, the Duke of Cumberland. The Prince Regent visited his uncle in 1783 and his subsequent patronage of the town for the next 40 years was central to the rapid growth – and the transition from Brighthelmston to Brighton.

WEDNESDAY 6th JULY 1994

The fourth stage of the Tour de France was the 204.5 miles from Dover to Brighton. The event, which also marked the opening of the Channel Tunnel, was watched by over three million spectators along the south coast. The riders pedalled down Ditchling Road, turned left at the south end of The Level, along Lewes Road and up Elm Grove, along Warren Road to Wilson Avenue where they went down to the seafront. The cyclists then headed to the Palace Pier, through Old Steine and Grand Parade for another lap commencing at the bottom of Elm Grove. The finish was a sprint along Madeira Drive. Unfortunately, the Barcelona Olympic gold-medallist Chris Boardman could not hold on to the yellow jersey long enough to wear it on home ground. Spaniard Francisco Cabello Luque won the stage while the disgraced Lance Armstrong was awarded a white jersey in the 'young rider classification'. The American went on to win the famous race seven consecutive times from 1999 after successfully beating cancer.

SATURDAY 7th JULY 2001

The very first *Big Beach Boutique* on Brighton seafront, between the piers, was attended by 35,000 revellers. The free concert drew fans from across Sussex to listen to global superstar DJ Fatboy Slim play to his hometown audience. The former Housemartin said seeing so many people had been an amazing experience and, as a Brightonian, it had been the "warmest" gig he had ever performed. The music was cut for five minutes mid-set amid concerns a section of the crowd was in danger of being washed away by the rising tide. Chief Inspector of Sussex Police Kul Verma commented: "The crowd was good-natured, the event was a success and once again the city proved its reputation as being a great place for a night out."

ONE OF MANY ANTIQUE SHOPS THAT THE LANES IS FAMED FOR. THIS ONE IS IN THE NARROW LANE CONNECTING BRIGHTON SQUARE AND MEETING HOUSE LANE. © ALAN WARES

WEDNESDAY 8th JULY 1936

Just a few days earlier, *The Times* had advertised the availability of the new flats in the stunning Art Deco 'skyscraper' on Brighton seafront. The 12-floor building – now known as Embassy Court – designed by architect Wells Coates, was one of the first modernist buildings to be constructed in the country. The ad included the following wonderful lines: '6 lifts wait to waft you to your door', 'And, of course – OCEANS OF OZONE everywhere!' Even more amusing was the price: 'Flats available from £125'!

MONDAY 9th JULY 2007

The Go! Team released the single *Grip Like A Vice*, from their second album, *Proof of Youth*. The Brighton-based six-piece's distinctive sound was conceived by band leader Ian Parton who wanted to create music incorporating 'Sonic Youth-style guitars, Bollywood soundtracks, double Dutch chants and old school hip hop'. This eclectic mix first saw the light of day when Parton recorded *Thunder, Lightning, Strike* in his parents' kitchen, or garage – depending on your source – in 2004.

FRIDAY 10th JULY 1908

Singer Donald Peers was born in Wales. Initially a house painter, he enjoyed his first BBC Radio performance in December 1927 with popular comedy duo, Clapham and Dwyer, and one of his songs – which he later became synonymous with – was *In A Shady Nook By A Babbling Brook*. Bumbling along, Peers served in World War II and got his big break in his one-man show at the Royal Albert Hall and the London Palladium in 1949. He was given his own radio show, *Cavalier of Song*, and at the height of his fame was receiving 3,000 fan letters a week. Peers died in a Hove nursing home in August 1973, at the age of 65.

THURSDAY 11th JULY 1765

Contrary to popular belief, the first royal visitor to Brighton was the Duke of Gloucester, who popped into the Castle Tavern Assembly Rooms in the evening and enjoyed breakfast at Stanmer House the following day.

MONDAY 11th JULY 1988

Former Brighton & Hove Albion chairman Mike Bamber died after a two-year battle with cancer. Bamber joined the board in 1970 and became head honcho three years later. In November 1973 he persuaded Brian Clough – who always regarded Bamber as the best chairman he worked for – to take over the reins but it was his appointment of Alan Mullery in 1976 that paved the way for the club's golden years.

FRIDAY 12th JULY 1850

Pool Valley was inundated by six feet of storm water. The area was the natural drainage point for the town's streams, and also where the Wellesbourne River (now underground) discharged into the sea.

SATURDAY 13th JULY 2002

A year after the first event, *Big Beach Boutique II* exceeded all predicted attendance figures as 250,000 partygoers descended on Brighton seafront. DJ Fatboy Slim's bash sent the city's public transport system into meltdown, overwhelmed emergency services, and human-gridlocked streets. By 3pm police realised they had a major incident on their hands and extra officers were drafted in from all over the county to cope with the gathering crowds. When Norman Cook bounced onto the stage at 9pm an unbroken sea of very happy faces stretched from the West Pier to the Palace Pier. A worried-looking Fatboy played a very restrained, but still uplifting, 90-minute set which ended with a blizzard of fake snow swirling down on the crowd from the West Pier. Brighton station was closed intermittently as crowds on the platform were squeezed on to the tracks. Despite the chaos, the crowd remained calm and good natured and the bash provided a much-needed shot in the arm for the city's economy after the preceding two months of miserable weather. Cook, aka Fatboy Slim, spent £100,000 of his own money to stage the event and also paid to clear up the 100 tonnes of rubbish.

THURSDAY 14th JULY 1831

The first Brighton 'trunk murder'. In North Steine Row, a now demolished street known locally as 'Donkey Row', John Holloway lured his estranged first wife Celia Holloway from her sister's house at Cavendish Place. He strangled the eight-months-pregnant Celia. Ann Kennett, Holloway's bigamously married second wife, helped Holloway cut off her head and arms, before dumping them in the privy of their lodgings at Margaret Street, with the remaining torso placed in a trunk and buried in a copse near Lover's Walk. Holloway, a labourer on the Chain Pier, described Celia, in his death-row confessions as 'a hideously deformed dwarf'. "I felt ashamed to be seen with her until after dark." He had felt aggrieved at being trapped into marrying her after she had become pregnant and the Overseers of the parish had imprisoned him for five weeks until he had agreed to support her. On December 21st, Holloway was hanged in Horsham. As he took the scaffold he addressed the crowd; "As sin has brought me to this untimely end, I would entreat you to be aware that there is not one among you who, if he follows a life of sin and folly, may not be brought to the same condition; for when you trifle with sin, you know not where it will end."

SATURDAY 15th JULY 1837

After much debate – six companies were in the running at one point – Parliament finally agreed to a direct railway line between Brighton and London. The necessary bill received the royal assent of Queen Victoria – just 25 days after she came to the throne. The 50-mile line was opened in two stages: 12th July 1841 – Norwood Junction, London to Haywards Heath; 21st September 1841: the final section from Haywards Heath to Brighton. There are seven tunnels.

MONDAY 15th JULY 1940

The first air raid of World War II flew over the two towns. The last was on March 22nd 1944 and during the conflict there were 1,058 siren warnings and 685 local alarms. A total of 56 air raids took place, 381 high-explosive bombs were dropped and incendiary bombs too numerous to tally. Civilian casualties were as follows; 198 fatalities, 357 seriously injured, and 433 slightly injured. Over 5,000 houses were damaged with 200 completely destroyed. Kemp Town, south Whitehawk and around the Old Steine incurred the worst of the Germans' wrath.

WEDNESDAY 16th JULY 1997

A meeting between Dick Knight and Bill Archer produced an agreed timetable to the change in ownership of Brighton & Hove Albion. The proposed groundshare with Millwall was not sanctioned so Priestfield Stadium, in Gillingham, Kent, would be 'home' for the next two years...

SUNDAY 16th JULY 2000

The godfather of soul James Brown performed at the Essential Festival at Stanmer Park.

FRIDAY 17th JULY 1908

George Larner triumphed in the ten-mile walk at the 1908 London Olympic Games. The 33-year-old only took up competitive walking five years earlier. A Brighton policeman, his Chief Constable was persuaded to give him time off to train for the event. After retirement, Larner became a respected race-walking judge and when he died, at the age of 73, many of his British records were still intact.

SATURDAY 18th JULY 1545

Francis I, King of France, made a somewhat feeble invasion of England. Admiral Claude d'Annebaut, with 200 ships and 26 galleys of the French navy, made his descent upon the Sussex coast landing at Brighthelmstone. An old print recording the attack shows houses burning on the coast, with the town beacon afire, and the men of Aldrington and Hove marching to the assistance of their neighbours. The French were driven off wherever they landed, often with greater loss than they inflicted. Two cannon balls, which may date from this attack, are preserved in the Hove Museum.

SATURDAY 18th JULY 2009

World War I veteran and the first British man to reach 113 years of age, Henry William Allingham passed away. Born on Saturday 6th June 1896 in Clapton, London, Henry was in the RAF during the Great War and designed new car bodies for the Ford Motor Company at their Dagenham plant – which had opened just three years previously – from 1934. He retired to Eastbourne in 1960 and his wife of 52 years, Dorothy, died in 1970. They had two daughters; Jean, who died aged 78 in 2001, and Betty. At the time of his death, Mr Allingham had seven grandchildren, 16 great-grandchildren, 14 great-great-grandchildren, and one great-great-great-grandchild.

WEDNESDAY 19th JULY 1905

The first of the Brighton National Speed Trials, held over three days, zoomed along between the Palace Pier and Black Rock. Sir Harry Preston persuaded the council to tarmac the surface of the road adjacent to the beach in order to hold motor racing events. The highest speed was 90.2 mph, achieved in a 90 horsepower Napier. The stretch was renamed Madeira Drive in 1909 and the event continues to this day.

THURSDAY 20th JULY 1972

The Times reported how a British Caledonian plane overshot the runway in Corfu yesterday, killing a woman in her eighties from Hove. The pilot realised there was a problem with an engine, reduced speed and overshot the runway, landing in the sea.

THURSDAY 21st JULY 2005

East Brighton College of Media Arts in Wilson Avenue, Whitehawk, closed due to poor results and falling pupil numbers. The truancy rate was almost nine times the UK average and the comprehensive – formerly known as Stanley Deason – was ranked 24th from bottom out of the 3,579 schools in England, according to data from the Department for Education and Skills (DfES).

FRIDAY 22nd JULY 1932

The 60-foot-wide Marine Drive was opened between Black Rock and Rottingdean. The first development at Black Rock was the gasworks, established in 1818/19 by the Brighton Gas Light and Coke Company. This was followed by terraced housing and a pub, the Abergavenny Arms in 1829. The years of erosion claimed the inn but was thwarted by the construction of the Undercliff Walk (see 04/07/1933). What remained of the Black Rock community was demolished for the construction of the Marina road interchange which opened in 1976.

MONDAY 23rd JULY 1313

Long before high streets and shopping malls, the best place to pick up your daily wares in Brighton was from the weekly Thursday market. The first of its kind was granted to the lord of the manor, John de Warrenne, Earl of Surrey, by Edward II and was probably held on the cliff-top between Black Lion Street and Ship Street, just east of the Townhouse.

SATURDAY 23rd JULY 1580

The Book Of All The Auncient Customs heretofore used amonge the fishermen of the Toune of Brighthelmston (sic) was the result of the dispute between the fishermen and landsmen (see 12/02/1579). Two copies of the book, in black ink on parchment, were made and described fishermen's net regulations, hook sizes, and various payments and taxes pertaining to the church. It had seven signatures and 83 'marks' from the town's principal inhabitants. The Arundel copy now sits at the British Museum and the other is preserved by Howlett Clarke solicitors in Ship Street.

SATURDAY 23rd JULY 1864

Built for the upper classes, the eight-storey Grand Hotel – with 30 miles of flooring and six miles of gas piping – opened for business; all 201 rooms were booked. Many famous guests have glided through the revolving doors – to stay in one of the eight single, 115 standard twin and standard double, 31 sea-view twin and sea-view double, 42 sea-view deluxe rooms or four sea-view suites, including the presidential suite – and include Napoleon III, President Kennedy and Ronald Reagan.

SATURDAY 24th JULY 1897

From this day until 1908, a steep-grade railway ran down the northern slope of Devil's Dyke to a point west of Poynings village. Some 275,000 passengers a year were carried by the two-car trains.

SATURDAY 24th JULY 1999

After two long years at Gillingham, Brighton & Hove Albion Football Club were finally back in Sussex. Withdean Stadium welcomed Nottingham Forest for the inaugural friendly match on this day. The Albion players arrived on an open-top bus, while the Brighton Silver Band played *Sussex By The Sea* as the teams ran out in front of a sell-out 5,891 crowd. There was a streaker (male) during the 2-2 draw, Gary Hart scored the first Withdean goal, and the first of hundreds of supporter litter-patrols began in earnest.

SATURDAY 25th JULY 1808

A Brighton institution, Hanningtons, welcomed customers at 2 North Street. Smith Hannington, who died in 1855, opened his first store to sell linen, drapery, haberdashery and hosiery. Six years later the shop was extended and by 1885 several other premises had been purchased resulting in employment for 300 locals. By the 1980s the vast department store – once known as the *Harrods of Brighton* – was past its prime. Competition from out-of-town rivals heaped pressure on its owners, the Hunnisett family, who eventually sold the store to London property investor Regina Estates for more than £20 million in September 2000. The following June, after 193 years of trading, customers were asked to leave the store for the last time.

SATURDAY 25th JULY 1992

Brighton resident Sally Gunnell claimed a gold medal in the 400-metre hurdles final at the Barcelona Olympic Games. She is the only woman ever to hold four major track titles concurrently – Olympic, World, European and Commonwealth – and following retirement from international athletics, she became a television presenter and motivational speaker.

SATURDAY 26th JULY 1783

The first races were held at Brighton Racecourse. A group of Brighton's most established inhabitants, including the Duke of Cumberland, Marquess of Queensbury and Earl of Egremont, set up the first races on an area of land called Whitehawk Down, which later became known as the Race Hill. In 1786, the Brighton Races were extended to four days and the first stand was erected in 1788, with a capacity of 24. Famous for its distinctive horseshoe shape, and reputation as one of the fastest tracks in the country for sprint races, Brighton Racecourse is one mile and four furlongs long, and contains an extended downhill ...

... section that rises for a 100-yard level finish. Brighton was granted more land in 1822 by a number of local landowners and as the racecourse grew in popularity the town's local authority had assumed full control by 1898. The 1920s saw the return of a London influence, and the arrival of gang culture that often sparked fighting and unrest that continued until June 1936 when the notorious 'Hoxton Mob' were arrested. The era inspired Graham Greene to write *Brighton Rock* in 1938, which was later adapted for the big screen. The present grandstand, opened in May 1965, accommodates 5,420 people, including 1,445 standing, and cost £400,000 to build.

MONDAY 26th JULY 1897

The foundation stone was laid on the site of the main Roedean School buildings. Founded by the Lawrence sisters, known locally as 'the Firm' – Dorothy, Millicent and Penelope – at 25 Lewes Crescent some 12 years earlier, the establishment aimed to provide more than the basic education available for women at the time. The school grew, taking in various buildings in the area, until the impressive Flemish-style structure was built on their Roedean Road playing fields. At the start of World War II, Roedean's pupils were evacuated to Keswick in the Lake District as the Army commandeered the school. The building became HMS Vernon, home to over 30,000 sailors attending the Mining and Torpedo School and working for the electrical branches of the Navy. As a result, Roedean is perhaps the only girls' school in the country to have an Old Boys' Association.

WEDNESDAY 27th JULY 1921

On the site where Boots now stands in North Street, the Regent Cinema – so called to reflect its association with the town – was opened to seat 3,000 filmgoers. Prior to the picture house, the historic Unicorn Inn – built 1597, demolished 1920 – had stood on the site for over 320 years. It was one of the first (if not the first) of a new breed of 'super cinema' picture palaces built after World War I. Costing £400,000, it had a restaurant with an orchestra, Ship Café and an upstairs dance hall, reputed to have one of the best sprung floors in the country. The venue re-opened in July 1929 complete with a British Acoustic Films (BAF) sound system, claimed to be the first sound-equipped cinema in Brighton and 38 years later the ballroom became a bingo hall. The building closed when the Kingswest opened at the bottom of West Street in April 1973. Virgin Records had one of their first record shops on the corner adjacent to the cinema before vacating in 1977.

MONDAY 28th JULY 1980

Great Britain hockey player Ben Hawes was born in Brighton. He represented Great Britain at the 2004 and 2008 Olympics, as captain, and is an elected member of the British Olympic Association Athletes Commission.

SUNDAY 29th JULY 1860

Rear-Admiral Sir John Hindmarsh died in London. He joined the Navy in 1793, was at the Battle of the Nile in 1798, being the only surviving officer on the quarter-deck of HMS *Bellerophon*, and gave orders which saved the ship from destruction. He was promoted to lieutenant in 1803, and had a distinguished career until the end of the Napoleonic Wars in 1815. In 1830 he was in command of HMS *Scylla* and was made a knight of the Royal Hanoverian Guelphic Order. He travelled to South Australia to become its first governor in December 1836 when he proclaimed the colony under the Old Gum Tree. He returned to England 18 months after disagreements regarding the location of the territory's capital. In September 1840 he was appointed lieutenant-governor of Heligoland – a small German archipelago in the North Sea – and held the position for approximately 16 years. He was knighted by Queen Victoria in August 1851 and retired to 30 Albany Villas, Hove, where he lived for many years.

MONDAY 30th JULY 1956

A British Pathe newsreel was issued featuring the 'Brighton Promettes'. From the early 1950s to the mid 1960s, six women were selected for the job of selling Brighton, appearing in film footage all over the world. The trainee models, who dressed like air hostesses, offered advice and answered questions from tourists, were described by one local newspaper as a 'walking information bureaux with sex appeal'. The Promettes, who operated from a small caravan between the piers, were the brainchild of the town's publicity director, ex-Fleet Street newspaperman Sidney Butterworth. The girls could speak Spanish, Italian, German or French, were taught how to walk, stand and even take their coats off properly!

THURSDAY 31st JULY 2006

The BBC website reported two men's arrest in connection with a 12-year-old's murder in Happy Valley... 39 years earlier. Sussex Police said one, aged 55, was from the Manchester area, and the other, aged 56, was from Brighton. The body of Keith Lyon – he had been stabbed – ...

... was found on a grass bank near a bridle path between Ovingdean and Woodingdean on May 6th 1967. The 1960s' murder inquiry was "arguably one of the biggest murder investigations ever seen in Sussex", the force said. Officers took fingerprints from more than 5,000 youths, and while there were a number of potential suspects, no-one was charged. On the day he was killed, Keith had gone to a shop, in his grammar school uniform, to buy a geometry set. He was stabbed 11 times in the chest, back and abdomen with a serrated kitchen knife which, along with other items relating to the case, were later mislaid, and found in 2002 by workmen in the basement of Brighton police station. The two men were cleared six months later.

AUGUST

SATURDAY 1st AUGUST 1805

The Brighton Union Bank opened at 6 North Street in the town. It was one of only two banks that survived the financial panic of 1825, and was the sole survivor just 17 years later. Barclays Bank took over in August 1894…

MONDAY 1st AUGUST 1836

One of the oldest of its kind in the country, St Mary's Hall was founded as a school for 100 boarding daughters of clergymen. Erected on nine acres of land given by the Marquess of Bristol, the curate of St Mary's Church also donated a thousand books to the new establishment. The school was extended in 1920 to admit the daughters of laymen.

FRIDAY 1st AUGUST 1930

Following Art Deco design, the Savoy Cinema in East Street welcomed film lovers for the first time. The 2,300-seat venue cost £200,000, had a Westrex sound system, 300-space underground car park, two restaurants, two cafés and a dance hall. The building replaced the recently demolished Brill's Baths which had begun life in 1786 as a 'Turkish baths'. Sake Deen Mahomed, one of the country's first prominent Asians, developed a 'shampooing' (massaging) service which became popular after several successful cures, especially of rheumatic problems; the walls were hung with the discarded crutches of cured patients. The Bengali published several books and pamphlets on his methods and was eventually appointed 'Shampooing Surgeon' to King George IV, an appointment continued by William IV. Mahomed died in 1851, aged 102, and is buried just to the west of the northern entrance of St Nicholas' Church.

MONDAY 2nd AUGUST 1937

Adrian Thorne was born in Hove. The forward waited over three years to make his Brighton & Hove Albion debut and eventually appeared for the first team while stationed in Colchester during his Army national service. On only his seventh league outing, the local lad banged in five goals against Watford! The attacker went on to score 44 times in 84 Albion starts – over four seasons – but never really had the opportunity to establish himself. He moved to Plymouth Argyle in 1961, Exeter City in 1963 and finally, Leyton Orient in 1965.

TUESDAY 3rd AUGUST 1787

Brighton's status as a fantastic place to be is not a recent phenomenon. *The Times* reported: "A correspondent observes that Brighton is now become [sic] the only place of fashionable levity in the kingdom. The

Prince is perfectly re-instated; and the resort to participate with him in the pleasures of that place exceeds common belief. It is indeed the capital in epitome; and the general topic of conversation is the Prince, and Mrs Corbyn on the Cliff."

MONDAY 3rd AUGUST 1868

Now part of the Royal Sussex County Hospital on Eastern Road, the Brighton Hospital for Sick Children began life at 178 Western Road. In 1870, the hospital moved to the disused Church Hill School in Dyke Road where it was reopened with 20 beds on July 14th 1871, by the Bishop of Chichester. A three-storey red-brick building was opened by Princess Alexandra on July 21st 1881.

SATURDAY 4th AUGUST 1883

At noon, the first quarter-mile stretch – extending from a site on the seashore opposite the Aquarium to the Chain Pier – of the Volk's Railway carried passengers for the first time. No sooner was the railway open than its creator, Magnus Volk, sought powers to extend it westwards to the town boundary. The council vetoed his proposition so he reversed direction and succeeded in getting permission to extend eastwards to the Banjo Groyne. The new line opened on April 4th 1884 using one car. The power output was 160 volts at 40 amps – more than sufficient to propel the two new cars along the 1,400-yard-long line – and the arrival of the second car allowed a five- or six-minute service throughout summer and winter. Black Rock Station was on an exposed outcrop with little to welcome passengers except the possibility of a walk along the 'White Cliffs of Old England' towards Rottingdean. Over the next 25 years more cars were added – to make a total of ten – to handle the million or so passengers the railway carried a year. The 1930 redevelopment of Madeira Drive saw the line cut back at the western end while at the other end – Black Rock – the council decided to build a new swimming pool on the land currently occupied by the station. In order to accommodate the new development the eastern end of the railway was shortened by a few hundred yards. The Brighton Corporation took full control of the railway in April 1940 and the association with the Volk family ceased. In 1961 new owners decided on a facelift and from 1962 cars started to appear in a new brown and yellow livery with VR and the Brighton crest applied to the sides. Cheap package holidays did little to help passenger numbers and the decision was taken to keep the railway running at least until its centenary in 1983 – and then to see what the future held. In the 1990s a new storm drain project caused great disruption to the eastern end of the line, the 1948 station was ...

... demolished, and the line shortened by another hundred yards or so to a temporary station. Volk's Railway survives as the oldest operating electric railway in the world and is much loved by locals and visitors alike.

SATURDAY 5th AUGUST 1826

The Royal Albion Hotel, designed by A H Wilds, opened its doors for visitors for the first time. Following the demolition of Russell House three years earlier, the town commissioners agreed to pay £3,000 to John Colbatch to preserve the site as an open space. The deal was delayed, and never concluded, and the hotel was built. The Albion became 'Royal' around 1847 but by 1900 it was in a very dilapidated condition and closed down. In 1913 it was purchased for £13,500 by the charismatic Harry Preston – the proprietor of the nearby Royal York – who restored the fortunes of the famous building attracting the famous figures of the day, especially in art, literature, sport and entertainment. Fire destroyed the top floors of the hotel in 1998 (see 24/11/1998).

WEDNESDAY 6th AUGUST 2002

Passengers on a Brighton to Edinburgh train were stranded after it hit a tree on the line after flooding had caused a landslide. The accident halted the service just north of Beattock, in Dumfries and Galloway. On the same day, a survey commissioned by branding and marketing specialists Superbrands, placed Brighton third, behind first-placed London and Manchester, as the 'Coolest Place in the UK'. Apparently, Croydon didn't feature in the top 500.

SATURDAY 6th AUGUST 2011

"Emotional", "exhilarating", "overjoyed", "speechless" and "about bloody time" were just a handful of the voxpops from one of the greatest and most memorable days in Brighton & Hove Albion's 110-year history. After 14 years in the wilderness the club finally had a home – and what a home it is. Fans flocked to the brand new American Express Community Stadium from around the world – some even hired an open-top bus for a scenic first journey – as the £93 million arena opened its doors for a league fixture, for the first time. The fitting opponents were Doncaster Rovers, the last visitors to the much-loved Goldstone Ground. A Will Buckley brace – including a last-minute winner – earned a 2-1 victory. Amazing.

THE SKELETAL FRAME OF THE WEST PIER. THIS MAY WELL BE A DISTANT MEMORY BY THE TIME YOU READ THIS.... © ALAN WARES

TUESDAY 7th AUGUST 1792

A two-day cricket match commenced at The Level that would see Brighton beat Hampshire. The eight-acre park space was once a marshy confluence of the London and Lewes Road streams and was laid out as a ground for the Prince of Wales and his brother the Duke of York's favourite sport in 1791. The last important fixture was played in August 1822. The Bat and Ball public house in Ditchling Road, in some way, shape or form, commemorates these early spectacles.

SATURDAY 7th AUGUST 1999

The day Albion fans everywhere had been waiting for; the end of the two-year exile in Gillingham! Mansfield Town were the first visitors to Withdean Stadium – the club's new temporary home – in the league. Darren Freeman helped himself to a hat-trick in the 6-0 thrashing, the first Albion player to score three times on his debut since the club's very first game in 1901. The majority of 5,882 fans in attendance went home very happy indeed.

SATURDAY 8th AUGUST 1981

The Mods were back in town… Nearly 80 were arrested, and seven ended up in hospital, as trouble broke out in Sloopy's club on Dyke Road. Chief Supt. Dennis Williams of Brighton police said in *The Times*; "It was a fast and furious fight but we managed to quell it quite quickly. We closed the disco down immediately and took the Mods, under escort, back to the seafront. Most of the scooterists were not in town looking for trouble."

MONDAY 9th AUGUST 2010

The residents of Brighton and Hove awoke from their collective slumber; some with sore heads, some fresh and ready for work, and some business owners smiling broadly, after a hugely successful Pride weekend. The celebration was the biggest in its 18-year history, with more than 160,000 revellers descending on the city. The parade left the seafront at 11 and made its way to Preston Park, where the event continued until the evening. Around 50 police officers, staff and supporters led the carnival parade for the seventh year running.

SATURDAY 10th AUGUST 1872

Brighton Aquarium – brainchild of Eugenius Birch, designer of the West Pier – was formally opened to the public by the mayor, Cordy Burrows. Erected on the approach roadway to the Chain Pier, the Aquarium necessitated the construction of a new sea-wall and promenade, the Madeira Road, which was commenced in 1869.

TUESDAY 11th AUGUST 1914

The last of the ten executions at Lewes Prison – since it opened in 1873 – occurred on this day. Percy and Maud Clifford were found, covered in blood, in bed at their lodgings at 57 North Road, Brighton in April 1913. Both had been shot and Maud was dead. The married couple had enjoyed a tempestuous relationship. Maud still worked as a prostitute, much to her husband's chagrin, and was, by all accounts, a very attractive lady. Excitable and jealous, Clifford had confided to a relative that he would one day kill his wife, and then turn the gun on himself. Percy Clifford enjoyed a hearty breakfast of three eggs, two rashers of bacon, and a pint of beer before the trapdoor gave way.

FRIDAY 12th AUGUST 1814

Long before obscure magicians descended on the town, artists welcomed strangers into their open houses as the unofficial 'Brighton Festival' took place on The Level. Each invitation instructed the bearer to: 'Bring a plate, knife, fork, drinking mug, be cleanly apparelled, not rise from the table during dinner, and be in their places for "¼ before Two o'clock".' The event celebrated the exile of Napoleon to Elba, an island of 12,000 inhabitants in the Mediterranean, 20km off the Tuscan coast. More than 7,000 Brightonians feasted, with their own cutlery, on roast beef and plum pudding. After the food the diners danced, played 'blind man's buff', and performed an early form of the conga all the way to Castle Square, before belting out God Save the King. The modern-day Brighton Festival owes nothing to the French Emperor.

THURSDAY 12th AUGUST 1819

To allay public fears regarding the town's new gas supply, the Brighton Gas Light & Coke Company illuminated a Prince of Wales's feathers sign on Mr Stone's shoe-shop at the corner of East Street and Steine Lane. It appeared to work as many residents embraced gas lighting thereafter.

TUESDAY 13th AUGUST 1793

Now home to a selection of hotels, offices, homes and a huge underground car park, Regency Square has changed beyond recognition since it was established as the first Brighton Military Camp in 1793. The Belle Vue Field was used for military reviews, fairs and shows, amongst other things, and approximately 10,000 soldiers were based there by the time it disbanded six months later. Becoming an annual event for about ten years after a second camp was established in the area, the vicinity proved popular with the area's ladies who were soon looking ...

... for husbands, and offering other nefarious wares. The Brighton Camps were described by Jane Austen in *Pride and Prejudice*.

MONDAY 14th AUGUST 1865

Sussex won the toss on the first day of the match versus Marylebone Cricket Club at the Royal Brunswick Ground, Hove – open from 1848 to 1871 – where Third and Fourth Avenues are situated today. With only four balls per over, the three-day contest finished a draw.

WEDNESDAY 15th AUGUST 1945

The residents of Brighton and Hove took to the streets to celebrate victory in Japan – the end of World War II was just a few weeks away. There was dancing in the streets, on the Pavilion Lawns, and the Aquarium terraces. Gigantic bonfires were lit on the beaches, with the unfortunate surviving beach huts the main source of fuel!

WEDNESDAY 16th AUGUST 1961

The University College of Sussex was established as a company in May 1959, and a royal charter was granted on this day for it to rise to full university status. The first 52 students were accepted in October and were temporarily accommodated at 235-237 Preston Road, with lectures given in the nearby Knoyle Hall. The original idea was mooted in December 1911 at a public meeting at the Royal Pavilion and a fund was started for the establishment of a university in Brighton. The project was halted by World War I and the money was used instead for books for the Municipal Technical College. The government approved the corporation's scheme for a university in June 1958, the first of a new generation of 'red-brick' universities. The university's student population expanded rapidly to about 1,500 in 1964/65 and up to nearly 4,200 in 1975/76. As of 2010, there were over 10,000 students, 2,000 staff, and the university was ranked in the top 5% of all universities worldwide.

MONDAY 17th AUGUST 1953

Lead singer of Dexys Midnight Runners, Kevin Rowland, was born in Wolverhampton. Regularly seen strolling around North Laine, the singer had huge hits in the 1980s with *Geno* and *Come On Eileen* – best British single at the 1983 BRITS – which was followed by *Jackie Wilson Said (I'm In Heaven When You Smile)*. When the band performed the single on *Top Of The Pops*, instead of an image of the American soul singer as a backdrop, Dexys performed in front of a huge photo of Jocky Wilson, the Scottish darts player!

FRIDAY 18th AUGUST 1933

Early film innovator James Williamson died in Hove, aged 77. Born in Kirkcaldy, the Scot headed to London in 1868 and opened his own pharmacy in 1877. In 1886 he migrated to the coast and built a film studio in Cambridge Grove, Hove. He originally processed film for other early filmmakers, and then began production of his own features, later moving into the film equipment manufacturing business with his son, an engineer. One of his most notable films was *The Big Swallow* (1901), in which a man appears to eat the film camera! Williamson approaches with his mouth open, walking into such an extreme close-up that his gaping mouth fills the screen, which goes black.

SUNDAY 19th AUGUST 1900

One of ten children, Gilbert Ryle was born in Brighton. He had a huge influence on the development of 20th-century analytic philosophy and argued that the science was like cartography. Competent speakers of a language, Ryle believed, are to a philosopher what ordinary villagers are to a mapmaker. This fascinating topic could fill dozens of pages.

SATURDAY 20th AUGUST 1960

John Barradell was born in London. The chief executive of Brighton & Hove City Council is a keen stamp collector and 'recreational cyclist', according to *Who's Who 2011*.

WEDNESDAY 21st AUGUST 1872

Aubrey Vincent Beardsley, the English illustrator and author, was born in Brighton. At the age of 15 he went to work in London, first for a surveyor and then in an insurance office. His first important commission, to illustrate Malory's *Morte d'Arthur*, came at the age of 20 and is widely considered to be a masterpiece. In 1894, he co-founded *The Yellow Book* – a leading journal associated with Aestheticism and Decadence, the magazine contained poetry, short stories, essays, book illustrations, and portraits – and for the first four editions he served as art editor. Most of Aubrey's images were done in ink and feature large dark areas contrasted with large blank ones, and areas of fine detail contrasted with areas with none at all. His style, overblown in manner and 'decadent' in subject matter, was dominant in England and the US during part of the 'great age of illustration'. Beardsley was active till his death from tuberculosis in Menton, France, at the age of just 25, in 1898.

TUESDAY 21st AUGUST 1962

The UK release date for *Jigsaw*. Shot almost entirely in Brighton, the murder mystery was based on Hilary Waugh's novel, *Sleep Long My Love*. The main crime took place at an isolated house – the fictional 1, Bungalow Road, Saltdean – and other local scenes included the police headquarters, then in Little East Street, an estate agent's in Queen's Road and Brighton institution Dockerills. The plot: a woman is found murdered in a house along the coast from Brighton. Local detectives lead an investigation methodically following up leads and clues mostly in Brighton and Hove, with some further afield.

SATURDAY 22nd AUGUST 1992

The Royal Pavilion hosted its first gay 'wedding'. Peter Gurling and Greg Wilson arrived at the iconic venue in a red BMW and were blessed – civil partnerships were legalised in 2004 – by Reverend David Miller who said of the union; "I don't think the Prince Regent would have batted an eyelid. We are here to witness the affirmation of two people's love for each other."

TUESDAY 23rd AUGUST 2005

Plans for a 600ft seafront observation platform won vital backing from English Heritage. The planning application for the proposed £20 million i360 tower at the land end of the derelict West Pier, on Brighton seafront, would be heard in October this year.

SUNDAY 24th AUGUST 2008

The final day of the inaugural – or, as it transpired, last – Beachdown festival just north of Brighton. A crowd of 10,000 camped at the site close to Devil's Dyke to see dozens of live locals acts and established groups including De La Soul, The Magic Numbers and The Maccabees. In spite of sporadic torrential downpours, the event was deemed a success but a mixture of poor organisation, bad ticket sales, the recession and outrageous performer costs proved to be the death knell of what could have become a very welcome addition to the festival calendar. Grace Jones was booked for the 2009 event on a reputed fee of £100,000 – a ridiculous amount for such a small festival.

SUNDAY 25th AUGUST 1861

The worst railway accident in Britain occurred five miles outside Brighton. Two excursion trains left Brighton only three minutes apart, followed just four minutes later by a regular train. The self-activated signal outside Clayton Tunnel failed to operate and confusion set in.

The second train stopped in the tunnel and attempted to reverse, only to be hit by the third train. Newspapers at the time were a bit too graphic in some circumstances. *The Times* reported: "…Another woman had her scalp completely torn off and both her arms broken. One man had his face crushed in such a manner as to force his eyeballs from his head." Twenty-two people lost their lives.

THURSDAY 26th AUGUST 2010

The paperback version of *The Brightonomicon*, a novel by Robert Rankin, was released in the UK. The book is set in a depiction of the city and is based on 'The Brighton Zodiac', a map consisting of carriageway constellations found in Brighton and Hove. It is the eighth and final book of a series, entitled the *Brentford Trilogy*, that are predominantly set in a west London public house. The story focuses on the grand high magus Hugo Rune (aka The Reinventor of the Ocarina, the Mumbo Gumshoe, the Hokus Bloke, and other incarnations) and his quest to solve the zodiac mystery, with the aid of his assistant, Rizla. *The Brightonomicon* was adapted into a 13-part full-cast audio drama in 2008 that aired on BBC7, and won *The Hub*'s 2008 Award for 'Best Comedy (Audio)'.

FRIDAY 27th AUGUST 1993

Five seriously injured children were rescued from the besieged Muslim sector of Mostar by Sally Becker. The 'independent' aid worker and artist, from Brighton, had spent six weeks in the area driving an ambulance carrying sick children, braving sniper fire to cross the front line with the intention of collecting a three-year-old boy with a heart complaint. The boy was dead but she managed to flee – in an old London ambulance – with five injured children. "My biggest hope is that this operation will open up the channels and we will be able to evacuate all injured children from every side of the war," said Ms Becker, 33. Sally first became interested in helping victims in the Bosnian war when she volunteered to drive aid convoys into the area. A very brave lady indeed.

THURSDAY 28th AUGUST 1913

Regarded as one of the finest British bridge players and writers, Terrence Reese was born in Epsom. The card game is played by four players in two competing partnerships – sitting opposite each other – and has two main parts: the Bidding (also called the Auction) and the Play. Reese also had a second career as a bridge author and journalist – a career that lasted throughout his life – and penned over 90 books on the subject. He married Alwyn Sherrington in 1970 and the couple resided in Hove, where he died of aspirin poisoning in 1996.

FRIDAY 29th AUGUST 1980

After just 18 months of operating services between Dieppe and Brighton, the 110-ton Boeing Flying Princess was withdrawn from service. The jet hydrofoil service, that reached speeds of up to 50 knots, reduced journey time to just two hours but was greatly affected by bad weather.

MONDAY 29th AUGUST 1983

Based at the former Rothbury Cinema – open between 1934 and 1964 – Franklin Road, Portslade-by-Sea, Southern Sound broadcast its first radio transmission. The commercial radio station, as Southern FM, was re-branded 'Heart' on June 22nd 2009, part of a network of 17 stations in central and southern England and north Wales that broadcasts local breakfast and drive time shows and simulcasts network programming at all other times.

FRIDAY 30th AUGUST 1833

Tragedy struck in Hove. Botanist Henry Phillips wanted to create a giant greenhouse, heated in winter, where he could grow trees, shrubs, plants and flowers from exotic parts of the world. The giant greenhouse, or Anthaeum as it became known, was to be constructed with a cast iron frame and completely clad in glass. A complete half sphere 164 feet in diameter and 80 feet high, the structure would be the largest dome in the world, larger than St Paul's or St Peter's in Rome. The site chosen was behind Adelaide Crescent, which at the time consisted of ten houses in the south-east corner closest to the sea. There was to be a grand official opening on September 1st 1833 and just two days earlier the internal scaffolding was removed. Crowds flocked to see the completed structure but that night – disaster. The complete dome collapsed; first the top came crashing down and then the ribs one after another like the sound of firing cannons. The tangled mass of broken and twisted cast iron – which inspired architect Joseph Paxton who, in 1850, was looking for ideas for his new Crystal Palace – was not removed for some 20 years until it was cleared for the building of Palmeira Square. Unbelievably, in 1945 Hove Council passed a plan to demolish Brunswick Terrace and Adelaide Crescent, for replacement with blocks of flats! As recently as 1966 a plan was considered to remove the Adelaide ramps for road widening along Kingsway. Fortunately, public outcry prevented both.

SATURDAY 30th AUGUST 1958

The first ITV broadcasting licence holder for the south and south-east of England, Southern Television, went on air at 5.30pm. The company –

who changed their name to Southern Independent Television in 1964 – beat eight other applicants for the contract. The first presenter on air was continuity announcer Meryl O'Keefe, followed by an outside broadcast fronted by Julian Pettifer.

THURSDAY 31st AUGUST 1944

Famous for his album covers, Roger Dean was born in Kent. Living in Brighton since 1972, Roger designed the now-classic Yes 'bubble' logo, which first appeared on the album *Close to the Edge*, and continued to create sleeves for the band until 1999.

TUESDAY 31st AUGUST 1999

The BBC reported that Brighton and Hove had competition for city status... from a village in Wales! St Asaph – with a population of 3,600 and famous as the birthplace of Lisa Scott-Lee from Steps and Liverpool legend Ian Rush – has a cathedral... In March 2012, St Asaph was finally awarded city status.

SEPTEMBER

THURSDAY 1st SEPTEMBER 1887

Nowadays a pleasant open-top bus ride from the centre of town, there was once a railway that snaked up to Devil's Dyke from Shoreham. Opening on this day, the track left the west coast line at Aldrington and ran alongside what is now Amherst Crescent, Rowan Avenue and Poplar Avenue, past Brighton & Hove Golf Course, to a station at Devil's Dyke Farm, which sat some 200 feet below, and over half a mile from the hotel. The 3.5-mile-long railway – served by Dyke Junction Halt, later Aldrington Halt, Rowan Halt in Rowan Avenue, and request stops at Golf Club Halt for the Brighton & Hove Golf Course – was a victim of increased motoring and closed on December 31st 1938.

FRIDAY 1st SEPTEMBER 1939

At 2am, the last tram ran from Upper Rock Gardens to the Old Steine. As the towns expanded, the public transport network required expansion but the system was inflexible and the corporation decided to replace trams with buses. After 38 years of almost accident-free service an estimated 52 million miles had been run, 629 million passengers carried, and a profit of £54,000 made by the Brighton trams.

SUNDAY 1st SEPTEMBER 1963

Sussex County Cricket Club were crowned inaugural winners of the Gillette Cup at Lord's. The 65-over tournament featured 17 first-class – and five minor – counties and Sussex beat Worcestershire by 14 runs after dispatching with Kent, Yorkshire and Northamptonshire en route to the final. Sussex's Jim Parks Jnr. was the competition's highest run scorer with 277.

SATURDAY 1st SEPTEMBER 1979

Brighton & Hove Albion enjoyed their first win in Division One. Peter Ward, Paul Clark and Brian Horton were all on target as Bolton Wanderers were dispatched 3-1 at the Goldstone Ground. It was the fourth game – two away defeats and one at home – and the result left Albion four places off the bottom on two points, one position above Tottenham Hotspur. The matchday programme featured pen pal requests from an Ipswich Town fan and an 18-year-old locksmith – a VfB Nufringen fan – from Germany.

SATURDAY 1st SEPTEMBER 2007

The first bus route operated by the Big Lemon – the 42X – ran from Brighton Station to Falmer Station. An eco-friendly company, the bright yellow vehicles run on 100% recycled bio-fuel made from locally-sourced used cooking oil.

MONDAY 2nd SEPTEMBER 1816

From *The Times*: "A gentleman of the name of Keane, who, with his family, resides at Hove, a village about a mile from Brighton, drove up to the post-office there in his curricle on Friday afternoon: he had three children (all boys) in the vehicle with him. Having alighted and got his letters, he directed his servant to take the reins, and drive slowly up North-street, and turn down West-street, at the bottom of which he (Mr Keane) would meet him. The man took his seat, and carefully obeyed his master's commands. He had nearly reached his destination, when, in passing a team in West-street, the curricle slightly grazed one of the horses, which instantly gave a tremendous kick, and dashed the carriage to pieces: the servant and children were thrown into the air, and fell with dreadful violence..." [all sic].

TUESDAY 2nd SEPTEMBER 1997

One of the biggest results in the Albion's history came off the pitch as the despised regime of Bill Archer, Greg Stanley and David Bellotti was finally replaced by Dick Knight, Bob Pinnock and Martin Perry, after two years of bitter fighting.

SATURDAY 2nd SEPTEMBER 2000

At the height of the 'superstar DJ era' – performers were paid thousands to play other people's records – *Stick It On* was born. Working at EMI record company at the time, Rob Drysdale decided to start his own club night where anyone could get behind the decks and play. Asking friends, initially, to pick their four favourite tracks for a 15-minute set, the night prospered, utilising internet technology for potential DJs to register their playlists. Ten years on and the idea has expanded to weddings, corporate events and DJ nights across the globe including New York, Sydney and Singapore. The inaugural *Stick It On* was held at the Hanbury Ballrooms on this day.

TUESDAY 3rd SEPTEMBER 2002

Fatboy Slim, aka Norman Cook, forked out £500,000 to become one of Brighton & Hove Albion's leading shareholders, giving him an 11 per cent share in the club's holding company. The incredibly generous act cemented his place in the hearts of Albion fans and earned him a car-parking space at Withdean.

MONDAY 4th SEPTEMBER 1939

In anticipation of systematic air-raids on the nation's capital, Brighton and Hove were designated an evacuation destination for children and hospital patients. The mass movement of people began in earnest today as 21,500 children arrived in Brighton and another 9,000 in Hove.

MONDAY 5th SEPTEMBER 1910

The Albion were crowned 'Champions of All England' on this day. Before Premiership winners faced that season's FA Cup winners in the traditional football season curtain raiser, the Southern League champions would face the Football League title winners for the Charity Shield. The season had already kicked off when Aston Villa – league champions six times in the previous 16 years – faced Albion at Stamford Bridge. In the 72nd minute Charlie Webb jinked past two defenders before powering home a rising cross shot. The Midlanders didn't win the league again for another 70 years.

SATURDAY 6th SEPTEMBER 1806

Not exactly the throbbing heart of Fleet Street, but number 8 Middle Street is where Brighton's very first newspaper hit the cobbles. H Robertson Attree and Matthew Philips, with Robert Sicklemore as editor, published the *Brighton Herald*. Attree went into partnership with William Fleet a couple of years later and moved the offices to Prince's Place after a brief sojourn in North Street. *The Herald* rapidly established itself as a leading weekly, and was the first newspaper to report the escape of Napoleon from Elba in 1815, the start of the French Revolution of 1830, and the arrival of Louis Phillipe at Newhaven in 1848. The name of the paper changed to the *Brighton Herald & Hove Chronicle* in 1902 and the *Brighton & Hove Herald* in November 1922. Sadly, the final edition – number 8,621 after 165 years – was produced on September 30th 1971 when *The Herald* was absorbed by the *Brighton and Hove Gazette*.

THURSDAY 6th SEPTEMBER 2007

After years of marches, letter-writing, protests, sit-ins, lock-outs, flower-sending, political party-forming, leaflet-dropping, postcard-distributing and petition-signing, Albion fans could finally, unequivocally, without question or chance of appeal, celebrate planning permission for the community stadium at Falmer. It had been a very long wait!

SUNDAY 7th SEPTEMBER 1783

Long before the 21st-century version was bemoaning British architecture and playing polo, the Prince of Wales made his first visit to Brighton. The eldest son of King George III, the profligate royal had just turned 21 and was the unofficial head of fashionable society; heir to the throne, George received the astonishing sum of £50,000 a year from his father – approximately £3 million in today's money! He commissioned famous designer John Nash to update his palace in 1815. Seven years later, the stunning, India-inspired Royal Pavilion was unveiled.

TUESDAY 8th SEPTEMBER 1874

Once a focal point of the beautiful vista across Brighton as trains pulled into the station, the imposing St Bartholomew's – now obscured by identikit hotels and a car park – welcomed parishioners for the first time. The huge church was built for the Reverend Arthur Wagner by local architect Edmund Scott for £18,000 and replaced a small mission church of 1866. The size of the church, and the fact that the 1,500 seats were all free, led to it being dubbed 'Wagner's Folly' by the locals. Supposedly constructed to the dimensions of Noah's Ark – 180 feet long, 58 feet wide and 140 feet to the top of the gilt metal cross – the building has the tallest nave of any parish church in the country.

SATURDAY 9th SEPTEMBER 1972

Despite being born in Brighton on this day, newsreader Natasha Kaplinsky's formative years were spent in Kenya, where she claims to have been fluent in Swahili. One of her first jobs was working in the press offices of Labour leaders Neil Kinnock and John Smith. Her paternal grandparents originated from Slonim (then in Poland, now in Belarus) and emigrated to South Africa in the 1920s. She served her apprenticeship in regional broadcasting before becoming anchor for *BBC News*, then *Five News*.

FRIDAY 10th SEPTEMBER 2010

Neil O'Maonaigh-Lennon, 30, from Harrow, north London, set off from Brighton to run anti-clockwise around the coast of Britain. The English teacher took about seven hours to complete the distance of 26 miles and 385 yards each day and wore a satellite tracking device to record his mileage. When each marathon was completed, a marker was placed on the road, from which point he started the following day. He completed a record-breaking 105 marathons in 105 days on December 23rd at the Palace Pier, where he was met by cheering crowds ...

... Neil went through several pairs of trainers in his bid to raise £10,000 for Cancer Research UK after both his grandfathers died from the disease. An amazing achievement.

TUESDAY 11th SEPTEMBER 2001

The world was reeling from the full impact of the terrorist attacks on the Twin Towers in New York City. As word filtered through to the TUC Conference audience at the Brighton Centre the initial reaction was 'it's a hoax'. The grim reality resulted in Prime Minister Tony Blair cancelling his speech amid security fears.

THURSDAY 12th SEPTEMBER 1907

The 'Camden Town Murder'. Bertram Shaw returned home to find his room locked. He entered to be greeted with the horrific sight of his fiancée, prostitute Emily Dimmock, lying naked on the bed, throat cut from ear to ear. Nothing was removed from the flat. It was a savage but skilful attack, with no apparent motive. A mystery, the case quickly became a sensation. Brighton-born Edward Hall was renowned for successfully defending many people accused of notorious murders – he became known as 'The Great Defender' – and represented the main suspect in the case, Robert Wood, who was almost certainly guilty; in the public's mind. Hall saved him from the gallows and the case remains unsolved to this day.

SATURDAY 13th SEPTEMBER 1930

Jason Winters was born in a council house in Stapley Road, Hove. He grew up in poverty and emigrated to Vancouver, aged 17, with his family when his sisters married Canadian soldiers. Standing at 6ft 2ins. Jason became a Hollywood stuntman, after a chance meeting, and thrived committing daring acts including canoeing up the Mackenzie River, crashing a hot-air balloon over the Rocky Mountains and then ditching a similar craft into the Atlantic in 1970. He was diagnosed with terminal cancer seven years later and decided to fight the disease with herbs. Jason said a combination of herbaline, red clover and chapparal took almost immediate effect and within nine weeks he was on the road to recovery – and to fame and fortune. He sold the blend rights to an American drug firm for $17 million and subsequently sold more than 13 million copies of his book, *Killing Cancer*. In 1985 Sir Jason was knighted in Malta as a Knight of Grace of the Order of Saint John. He died on December 12th, 2004 in Las Vegas.

SUNDAY 14th SEPTEMBER 1941

World War II was raging across Europe and the beaches of Brighton and Hove swapped candy floss and sunbathing for sandbags and barbed wire. Bombs had been dropped intermittently throughout the summer but today saw the worst of the hostilities. Twenty high-explosive devices were offloaded over Kemp Town with one landing on the Odeon cinema, which was packed with excited children. Four perished, along with two adults, while 20 people were injured. Bombing occurred sporadically throughout the conflict and barely a few days would pass without an aerial bombardment.

FRIDAY 15th SEPTEMBER 1961

It was the start of the weekend and as revellers poured into Brighton's town centre for a night of dancing, a gruesome tragedy was unravelling three floors above the Blue Gardenia nightclub in Queen Square. Alerted by the club owner's nanny, police arrived and shone their torches through the glass doors into the bedroom where Harvey Holford was sitting up in bed with his arm around his 21-year-old wife, Christine. Their heads were together and they appeared to be asleep. On closer inspection, her face was bloodstained and her right eye wide open. She had been shot three times in the head – through the front of the lower jaw, right temple and left ear – and three times in the body. Holford was deeply unconscious from an overdose of the barbiturate Seconal, with a gun by his side. Known as the 'king of Brighton', he owned the Whisky-A-Go-Go coffee bar, the Calypso Club and the Blue Gardenia Club, all located in the same building at 4 Queen Square. In July 1960, in the face of parental opposition, 31-year-old Holford and the teenage Christine eloped to Scotland where they planned to marry. They finally tied the knot in the November and a daughter, Karen Lesley Tracey, was born in May 1961. Outwardly, the couple seemed happy enough at first, although she was quickly unfaithful to Holford; soon after their daughter's birth he caught his wife kissing the Blue Gardenia's part-time barman. This wasn't Christine's first misdemeanour – and certainly wasn't the last. A hopeless flirt, her actions increasingly upset her husband. She once told a club-goer that Holford was "damaged goods"; his mother informed him – aged nine – that he was fathered by a lover, and not her husband. A month before she died, Christine met Conservative MP Richard Reader Harris on holiday and was introduced to millionaire tycoon John Bloom. She became infatuated with Bloom, who promised her swish apartments and £20,000-a-year to be his mistress. Christine taunted her husband over Bloom's superior performance in bed and Holford savagely assaulted her. She recovered ...

... sufficiently to celebrate her 21st birthday on September 1st when Harvey took the couple to see *Talk of the Town* in London. On the way home, she showed him a letter explaining that she was to leave him… An almighty row raged and hurtful words were exchanged culminating in Christine's last utterance: "You can stop crying about Karen because she is not yours." Holford later said: "I felt something go. I snatched a gun out of the cupboard and shot her. I just fired at her." It took Holford 82 hours to regain consciousness. He served three years in prison, changed his name to Robert Keith Beaumont, became an estate agent, stood as an independent candidate for Brighton Pavilion in 1974, set up the Maria Colwell Memorial Fund, and died of leukaemia, aged 77.

THURSDAY 15th SEPTEMBER 1977

The 'big wedding cake', as it is known to some Brighton and Hove residents, revolved its doors to the public for the first time. The nine-storey Amex House – European operations centre of the American Express Corporation – covers 300,000 square feet of office space and is home to over 2,000 workers in Edward Street, Brighton. In 1890, the quarter-mile stretch from the bottom of the road by the Royal Pavilion and up past the two towns' biggest employer's home was served by a staggering 26 public houses – one every 17 yards!

THURSDAY 16th SEPTEMBER 1841

The Brighton Gazette: "The Brighton Terminus is a beautiful structure, and with the iron sheds in the rear, will not suffer from comparison with any railway terminus in existence. The offices and waiting rooms are most commodious, and are furnished with every convenience for passengers. Gas fittings for the whole terminus have been put up by Brighton & Hove General Gas Company."

THURSDAY 16th SEPTEMBER 1937

Popular actress Bella Emberg, famous for her Blunderwoman character on *The Russ Abbot Show*, was born in Hove. She also appeared on *The Benny Hill Show*, *Softly, Softly* and *Z Cars*.

THURSDAY 16th SEPTEMBER 1967

Re-opening as the Holiday Inn, the Bedford Hotel – 17 storeys and 127 rooms – originally welcomed guests in 1829. Charles Dickens stayed here while penning *Dombey and Son*, which was published in monthly instalments between October 1846 and April 1848. The story concerns Paul Dombey, the wealthy owner of a shipping company, whose dream ...

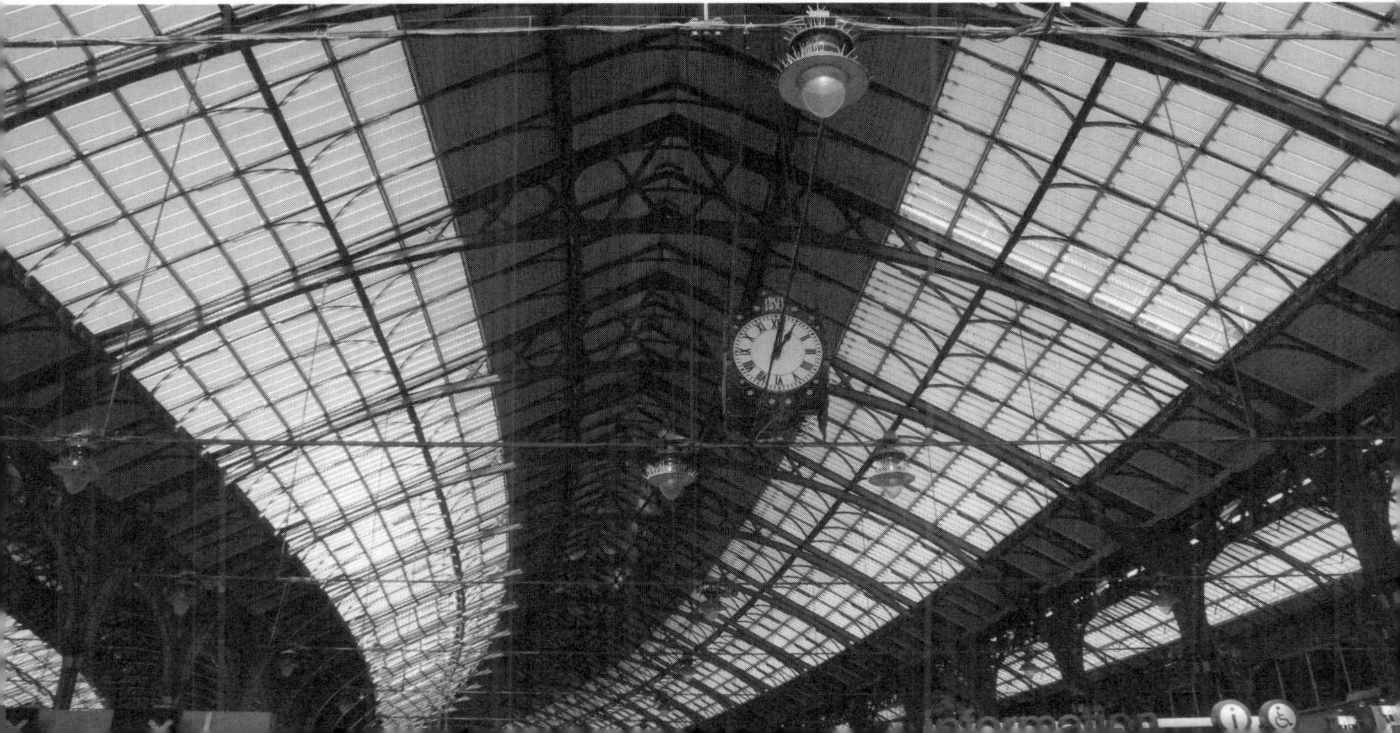

BRIGHTON STATION'S VERY EXPENSIVE ROOF. © ALAN WARES

... is to have a son to continue his business. His wife dies, clasping her little daughter Florence. This child, neglected by her proud, cold father, tries vainly to win his love, but he, with all his hopes and his affection centred upon his son, finds no place in his heart for Florence...

MONDAY 17th SEPTEMBER 1973

Published in the *Gay Times* this week: "...by the 1930s pubs with a lesbian or gay clientele were flourishing – among these, the Star of Brunswick in Brunswick Street West and Pigott's bar at the St James's Tavern in Madeira Place were especially popular." Playwright and local historian John Montgomery later wrote; "From London in the thirties we used to roar down to Brighton in fast sports cars... There was also the New Pier Tavern, long since gone, with its noisy honky-tonk piano, thick atmosphere of tobacco and sprinkling of red-coated, pink-faced guardsmen, and sailors from Portsmouth."

WEDNESDAY 18th SEPTEMBER 1822

Forerunner of the West and Palace, the Chain Pier's construction commenced. Completed in September 1823 at a cost of £30,000, the deck of the pier was 1,154-feet long and 13-feet wide and supported by chains suspended from four cast-iron towers spaced at 260-feet intervals on wooden piles driven into the seabed. Access to the pier was either via the foot of the cliff from the Old Steine, or down a flight of steps from New Steine.

MONDAY 19th SEPTEMBER 1977

Prime Minister James Callaghan formally cut the ribbon at the Brighton Centre. Essential to Brighton and Hove's economy, the building – at a cost of £9 million – was designed by Russell Diplock. Brighton has been a major conference centre since the annual meeting of the British Association for the Advancement of Science at the Royal Pavilion and Town Hall in 1853. The first political party conference was held by the Conservatives in 1875. Labour arrived in town 46 years later.

SATURDAY 20th SEPTEMBER 1975

Famous for its beautiful architecture, *The Times* reported on Brighton celebrating European Architectural Heritage Year by mounting an exhibition on the state of the town in 1975. The article also highlighted a 'delicious' section that shows grandiose plans that came to nothing, including a 'vast marine palace, an Oriental quarter, and zoological gardens where privileged tigers lived, naturally, in house with onion domes and minarets'.

SATURDAY 20th SEPTEMBER 1980

Olympic champion Steve Ovett – who had collected 800-metre gold, and 1,500-metre bronze at the Moscow Games less than two months earlier – inaugurated the all-weather running track at Withdean Stadium, closely followed by hundreds of local schoolchildren.

THURSDAY 20th SEPTEMBER 2007

One of Brighton's best clubs became a victim of the new UK licensing laws. The Sussex Arts Club, in Ship Street, was a haven for locals, and celebrities, to relax undisturbed for the preceding 15 years. Founded in 1994 for people who work in the arts, or have an interest in them, the club made use of a Grade II listed Georgian building in the heart of the Lanes. With two bars and a large ballroom – complete with a stunning atrium, atmospheric lighting and constantly refreshed new works from local artists – the club hosted a huge variety of events including famous club nights Da Doo Ron Ron and Family Funktunes. The truly unique venue – which was also home to seven individually-designed bedrooms named after Brighton celebrities, including the Wilde, Olivier and Greene rooms – is now part of the adjacent hotel. One of many venues sadly lost to changing hours, and changing tastes.

TUESDAY 21st SEPTEMBER 1841

The first train chuffed into Brighton Station. By the 1830s, Brighton was the most popular seaside resort in Britain. After the success of the Liverpool & Manchester Railway, a group of businessmen decided to build a railway between the town and London. Robert Stephenson was asked to advise on the best possible route and whittled the contenders down to two possible options; George Rennie's direct line between London and Brighton, and George Bidder's route that favoured steep gradient and tunnel avoidance. Rennie's proposal only involved the construction of 39 miles of new track but included four long tunnels at Mertsham (2,180 yards), Balcombe (800), Haywards Heath (1,450) and Clayton Hill (1,730) and a viaduct across the Ouse valley near Ardingly. Building started in July 1838 and the coal-burning locomotives made it impossible to keep the whitewashed tunnels – lined with corrugated-iron sheeting to avoid water falling on open third-class carriages – clean. Over 3,500 men and 570 horses were used to build the railway, which was completed in September 1841 at a total cost of £2,634,059 (£57,262 per mile). In 1843, third-class tickets were reduced to 3s 6d and in the forthcoming six months, 360,000 people arrived in the town by train. Between 1841 and 1871, the population of Brighton increased from 46,661 to 90,011, making it the fastest growing town in ...

... Britain. The city is now part of the Brighton/Worthing/Littlehampton conurbation which has a population of 461,181 (2001 census), making it the 12th largest conurbation in the UK after Greater Belfast. The largest conurbation on the English Channel coast, in either England or France, around one in three of Sussex's population live within its boundaries. The area is also the UK's most densely populated major conurbation outside of London with 4,901.5 people per km^2. This is primarily due to its tight boundaries between the South Downs national park to the north, and the Channel to the south.

SATURDAY 21st SEPTEMBER 1991

A healthy contingent of Brightonians – many on their return from Brighton & Hove Albion's 3-1 defeat at Derby County – were among the sell-out White Hart Lane crowd for Chris Eubank's keenly anticipated re-match with London's Michael Watson. An incredible fight – for the vacant WBO world super-middleweight title – went all the way. In the 11th round, Watson – ahead on points and seemingly on the verge of a stoppage victory – knocked Brightonian Eubank down with a right hook. Moments later he was back on his feet, and Eubank connected with a devastating uppercut which caused Watson to fall back and hit the back of his head against the ropes. The referee stopped the fight in round 12, and then Watson collapsed. A total of 28 minutes elapsed before Watson received treatment in a hospital neurosurgical unit. He spent 40 days in a coma, had six brain operations to remove a blood clot, was in intensive care and rehabilitation for a year, and was wheelchair-bound for a further six. Watson sued the British Boxing Board of Control for negligence and won damages reputedly around £1 million. In 2003 he completed the London Marathon over six days and was awarded an MBE the following year.

TUESDAY 21st SEPTEMBER 2010

Famous Brighton resident Annie Nightingale was presented with the 'Longest Career as a Radio Presenter (Female)' award by former Oasis frontman Liam Gallagher in London. Born in the capital in 1942, 'The Queen of Breaks' has enjoyed a career spanning four decades, including a weekly radio show on Radio 1. She describes Jimi Hendrix as "charming", Jim Morrison "a bit of an arse" and Marc Bolan "hilarious". Many big names from the music business have attended epic parties at her house in Brighton. Keith Moon and Pete Townshend were regulars, as were Eric Clapton and Rod Stewart, and in later years the Happy Mondays popped in. In 1992 she hosted a rave there that lasted six days. At the age of 19 she had the first of her two children, who went on to become manager of Primal Scream. Remembering her introduction to live broadcasting, Annie said it could have ended very differently: "When I took the wrong record off and caused eight seconds of dead air on my very first Radio 1 show, I thought that was the beginning and end of me."

THURSDAY 22nd SEPTEMBER 1910

The oldest continuously operating purpose-built cinema in Britain, The Duke of York's, opened its film-loving doors. One of Brighton's first picture palaces – and also one of the first in the world – the one-screen venue once seated 800 patrons. Built on the site of the Amber Ale Brewery and retaining many of its original features, The Duke's tagline for many years was; 'Bring her to the Duke's, it is fit for a Duchess'. Now an art house cinema – with 283 seats – the giant 'can can dancer' legs that protrude from the roof came from the 'Not The Moulin Rouge Theatre' in Oxford.

THURSDAY 22nd SEPTEMBER 2005

Housewives' favourite Des Lynam was named as the late Richard Whiteley's replacement on *Countdown*. He moved to Brighton from Ireland aged six, attended Varndean, worked in insurance, and took his first broadcasting job at BBC Radio Brighton in his mid-20s. Best known as the anchor for *Match of the Day* from 1988 to 1999, Des also hosted *Grandstand* and *Sportsnight* – and many other programmes including some on ITV – before retiring from presenting live sport after the Euro 2004 football championships.

THURSDAY 23rd SEPTEMBER 1999

One hundred people were chosen to represent Brighton and Hove as the towns planned their bid to become a city for the next millennium. The '100 Faces' project aimed to promote the area's heart and soul and the featured people ranged from a baby not yet born to a 99-year-old retired policeman.

THURSDAY 24th SEPTEMBER 1992

Police destroyed confidential files containing personal details about gay men in Brighton. Compiled from questionnaires issued during the inquiry into Peter Halls' murder two years earlier, the documents were shredded at John Street police station in front of representatives from the OUTrights group. During the original murder inquiry, police collected 616 questionnaires from gay bars and clubs, of which 148 ...

... were considered relevant and entered onto the system. Arthur Law, OUTrights spokesman, told the *Brighton & Hove Leader* it was a victory for the gay community; "The question is one of sensitivity around people's sexuality... I believe the police have every good intention and want to restore confidence."

WEDNESDAY 25th SEPTEMBER 1872

Sir Charles Blake Cochran was born in Brighton. Educated at Oxford, he became an actor and made his first appearance in New York. He produced musical revues and spectaculars in the 1920s, and collaborated regularly with Noël Coward to produce Coward's famous plays and musical comedies. Cochran was knighted in 1948 and died in January 1951 after being trapped in a bath full of scalding water.

TUESDAY 26th SEPTEMBER 2000

The Brighton Centre hosted the annual Labour Party conference. Prime Minister Tony Blair promised education spending would continue to increase if his government won a second term. "For 18 years Britain suffered chronic under-investment in our public services. It held people back – it reduced opportunity."

TUESDAY 27th SEPTEMBER 1859

Fred Lillywhite's team beat Lower Canada by eight wickets in Montreal, Quebec, the very first victory – and cricket match – on foreign soil by an English side. It was the first of five official tours matches organised by the Hove-born cricket entrepreneur. In 1848, still not yet 20, Lillywhite produced the first edition of his *The Guide to Cricketers* – in many respects, the forerunner of *Wisden Cricketers' Almanack*, which was published until the year of his death in 1866.

TUESDAY 28th SEPTEMBER 2004

A dead horse was dumped near Brighton station while two calf carcasses were placed near the Labour Party's conference at the Brighton Centre. Coincidentally, a pro-hunt march took place simultaneously on the seafront. RSPCA head of press Ann Grain said: "This is a mindless and appalling act which serves no purpose. Whoever has done this cannot have any respect for animals."

WEDNESDAY 28th SEPTEMBER 2005

Three people were arrested after obscenities were written on a Countryside Alliance stand at the Labour Party conference. A spokesman for the organisation put the cost of the damage at an estimated £3,000. "It is going to cause us a certain amount of inconvenience as we are supposed to be taking this stand to the next Conservative Party conference in Blackpool on Saturday," said a spokesman.

WEDNESDAY 29th SEPTEMBER 2010

The Brighton Tsunami (yes, really) American Football Club were busy recruiting new players at the University of Brighton Freshers' Fair. Formed in 2003, they originally signed players from both the University of Brighton and the University of Sussex but a single institution rule was enforced from the 2010/11 season.

TUESDAY 30th SEPTEMBER 1975

The West Pier closed. Possibly one of the town's biggest-ever failings, a public inquiry was then held into the 109-year-old pier's future in 1971, but when the council's policy committee recommended that demolition should not be opposed in December 1974, a strong protest group led by John Lloyd conducted a long campaign which, armed with a 5,000-signature petition, persuaded the council at least to postpone a decision on the pier.

OCTOBER

SUNDAY 1st OCTOBER 1837

One of the country's most prolific hangmen, James 'Jemmy' Botting, died on the corner of Codrington Place and Montpelier Road in Brighton. He was the executioner at Newgate Prison in London from 1817 to 1819 and claimed to have despatched 175 men and women during his time as a terminator. An exponent of the short drop – just a couple of feet which would prolong the criminal's agony as they 'danced' at the end of the rope – Botting's executions were predominantly undertaken in public, sometimes in front of 100,000 'spectators'. In his later years, Botting became partially paralysed and this forced him into retirement on a state pension and the occasional free drink in pubs when he told gruesome stories. Many Brightonians refused to be associated with him and legend has it that he fell out of his wheelchair and no-one came to his aid, thus leaving him to die.

SATURDAY 1st OCTOBER 1932

Brighton & Hove Albion club secretary Albert Underwood famously forgot to register the club for exemption from the four qualifying rounds of the FA Cup! As a result, County League Shoreham visited the Goldstone and were promptly hammered 12-0! Arthur Attwood plundered a double hat-trick.

SUNDAY 2nd OCTOBER 1904

Author Graham Greene was born in Hertfordshire. Catholic religious themes are at the root of much of his writing, especially the four major Catholic novels: *Brighton Rock, The Power and the Glory, The Heart of the Matter* and *The End of the Affair*. Greene suffered from bipolar disorder and his parents were first cousins.

WEDNESDAY 3rd OCTOBER 1990

The Albion revealed that Harry Enfield's 'Loadsamoney' character filmed a sketch for his new TV comedy programme behind the North Stand goal with groundsman Frankie Howard as an extra!

WEDNESDAY 4th OCTOBER 1769

Dr John Awsiter opened the first baths in Brighton in a building on the south-western side of Pool Valley. There were six cold baths, a hot bath, a showering bath and a sweating bath.

WEDNESDAY 4th OCTOBER 1837

Queen Victoria made her first visit to Brighton. The monarch was greeted by a floral arch at Preston Circus and an equally flowery amphitheatre at the North Gate of the Royal Pavilion. In February 1842, she visited with her new husband, Albert, and the following year landed at the Chain Pier from France. Surprisingly, and unlike her two predecessors, Victoria was not particularly enamoured with Brighton and complained that; "The people are very indiscreet and troublesome here really, which makes the place quite like a prison."

TUESDAY 4th OCTOBER 2005

Probably the most amazing headline ever connected with Brighton & Hove Albion Football Club was printed in *The Argus*; "Maradona Eyes Up Albion"! It was reported that the Argentine – probably the best footballer of his generation – was eyeing up a takeover bid with his compatriot Ossie Ardiles. Chairman Dick Knight said of the revelation: "I believe it is distinctly probable that all sorts of people would be interested in the Albion when we get our stadium."

MONDAY 4th OCTOBER 2010

Sir Norman Wisdom passed away at 6:46pm at Abbotswood nursing home on the Isle of Man, aged 95. The lifelong Albion fan became a professional entertainer at 31 and enjoyed a phenomenal rise to the top after an initial stint as the straight man to the magician David Nixon where he adopted the outfit that would remain his trademark: tweed flat cap askew, with peak turned up, an ill-fitting suit, a crumpled collar and a mangled tie – 'the Gump'. Wisdom was a cult icon in Albania. Known as 'Mr Pitkin' after the character from his films, he visited the post-Stalinist country in 2001, which coincided with the England football team playing Albania in the city of Tirana (of which Norman was granted the freedom in 1995). His presence at the training ground eclipsed that of David Beckham and he appeared on the pitch wearing a half Albania and half England shirt. He also famously re-wrote the words to *Good Old Sussex By The Sea*, the brass band tune the Albion run out to before each home game.

THURSDAY 5th OCTOBER 2000

Brighton & Hove Buses were nominated for two categories at the prestigious 'Bus Oscars' at the London Hilton Hotel in November.

SATURDAY 6th OCTOBER 1866

The West Pier was opened by the mayor, Henry Martin. Construction commenced in April 1863 using Eugenius Birch's cast-iron screw piles, and took three years to complete at a cost of £27,000. Stretching for 1,115 feet out to sea, the structure initially had only two square kiosks at the entrance, two octagonal kiosks with minarets in the centre, and four more octagonal kiosks at the corners of the large pier-head platform which also had some windshields. Among the original attractions was a miniature cannon fired by the sun at midday, and the skull of a whale washed ashore in January 1882. In 1893, the pier head was widened and a large pavilion was erected, seating 1,400, and a landing stage was added at the same time. With the outbreak of World War II, and the changed circumstances of its aftermath, the fortunes of the West Pier began to decline. As the fashion for foreign holidays took hold in the 1950s and 1960s, the neglected pier fell into disrepair. Declared unsafe, the grand old structure was closed to the public in 1975. Almost immediately the battle to restore the pier to its former glory began but it wasn't until 1998, with the granting of a major Lottery award, that the goal seemed achievable. Sadly, hopes of restoration were dashed when the pier – by now full to the brim with nearly three decades of incendiary seagull and pigeon droppings – was destroyed by fire in 2003. A year later, former world middleweight boxing champion Chris Eubank expressed an interest in renovating the structure saying; "...I don't even need the Heritage Lottery Fund – I will raise the finance myself."

TUESDAY 6th OCTOBER 1891

Political heavyweight Charles Stewart Parnell died of a heart attack, in his wife's arms, at 10 Walsingham Terrace, Hove, aged just 45. Regarded as one of the most extraordinary figures in Irish and British politics, Parnell played a part in the process that undermined his own Anglo-Irish caste; within two decades absentee landlords were almost unknown in Ireland. He created – single-handedly – the first modern disciplined political party machine, holding together all strands of Irish nationalism, and harnessing Irish-America. Though an Anglican, his funeral at Glasnevin Cemetery in Dublin was attended by more than 200,000 people. Such was his notability that his gravestone of uncarved Wicklow granite, erected in 1940, reads only 'Parnell'.

WEDNESDAY 7th OCTOBER 1959

High-trouser-wearing destroyer of deluded dreams, Simon Cowell, was born in Brighton. His older brother Tony, a radio broadcaster and television showbiz correspondent, claims a young Simon worked as a runner on Stanley Kubrick's *The Shining* but did not get along well with his colleagues or bosses. He is also responsible for a few chart 'hits' through his *X-Factor* and *Pop Idol* franchises. Thanks a bunch.

THURSDAY 8th OCTOBER 2009

Brighton Housing Trust staff – who work with the city's homeless – slept on the street in Queen's Road to highlight the proposed 20% cut to their salary and increase in working hours.

SUNDAY 9th OCTOBER 1955

One of Brighton's finest sons was born – Steve Ovett. The former middle distance runner was 800m gold medallist at the 1980 Olympic Games in Moscow and set world records for 1,500m and one mile. To this day, he holds the UK record for two miles which he set in 1978. Educated at Varndean, the youngster showed great promise as a footballer but gave it up to concentrate on athletics. At 18 he won the silver medal at 800 metres in the 1974 European Athletics Championships. He raced into the world spotlight in 1977 when, at the inaugural IAAF World Cup in Dusseldorf, he unleashed an astonishing kick with 200 metres to go to leave Olympic 1,500-metre champion John Walker, and the rest of the field, for dead. His famous rivalry with Seb Coe began the following year, but his greatest moment over his rival came when Ovett beat the Conservative MP by three metres in the 800m Moscow final. Coe picked up the 1,500m gold a few days later as Ovett collected the bronze. He moved to Scotland to start a family with wife Rachel after finishing competitive athletics. He then moved to Noosa, Australia as the resultant offspring showed aptitude for their father's discipline and required better weather for training. Modest throughout his career, his four children did not even know he was an Olympic champion, until one of their teachers mentioned it. In 2005 he completed the Kokoda Trail – a 96-kilometre trek through rainforest that links the north and south coasts of Papua New Guinea – for charity. "I agreed to do it on the phone, and then I looked it up on the internet. It takes nine days! I think I have always been slightly unaware of how that era, or the impact that era had on the general public and perhaps even the world... I got to a village and they put on a sing-sing, a major dance, because the mayor of the village happens to be an ex 5,000 and 10,000 metre runner from Papua New Guinea, one of the very few runners they have ever sent to the Commonwealth Games. And he knows Steve Ovett, and this was his way of showing his respect and honour for someone like me turning up at the village. And that just completely blows me away. I just think I do not deserve this," explained the Olympic champion.

MONDAY 10th OCTOBER 1977

Bing Crosby, one of the first truly global megastars, performed on stage for the last time, at the Brighton Centre, before passing away just four days later in Madrid, aged 74. With 1,077,900,000 cinema tickets sold, Crosby is the third most popular actor of all time, behind Clark Gable and John Wayne. A strong proponent of smoking marijuana when it was legal in the US, he fathered seven children by two women and his daughter, Mary, played Kristin Shepard in the American soap *Dallas*, famously shooting JR Ewing in the summer of 1980.

FRIDAY 11th OCTOBER 1968

There was a time when Churchill Square was not an undercover shopping mall that attracts millions of shoppers a year. On this day, a concrete homage to the decade – built for the incredible sum of £9 million – was unveiled: home to 70 stores and two supermarkets with the 'centrepiece' of the East Germanesque development a 30-foot concrete sculpture, the 'Spirit of Brighton', by William Mitchell.

SATURDAY 12th OCTOBER 1912

Standing 30-feet tall – at the seafront boundary of Brighton and Hove – the Peace Memorial was unveiled by the Duke of Norfolk. The listed memorial bears a portrait of Edward VII, the arms of the two boroughs, and the following inscription: 'In the year 1912 the inhabitants of Brighton and Hove provided a home for the Queen's Nurses, and erected this monument in memory of Edward VII and as a testimony of their enduring loyalty.'

MONDAY 12th OCTOBER 1931

The Times reported a murder in Hove... "Some remarkable evidence is expected to be given at the inquest at Hove today on the body of Walter Applegate, a hairdresser, who was found shot in his shop in Church-road, Hove on Saturday morning. Applegate, who was a well-known Freemason, would have been an important witness at the resumed inquest on October 21st on the body of Laura Emily Shinn, 37, who collapsed while walking with Applegate at Patcham and died from cyanide of potassium poisoning... On Saturday morning Applegate informed the Hove police that he had been the victim of a robbery, and Chief Inspector Bowden and other police officers visited him. They had previously been told by the Brighton police, who were inquiring into Miss Shinn's death, that, in consequence of information they had received, they wished to have another interview with Applegate. ...

ERECTED IN 1968, WILLIAM MITCHELL'S 'SPIRIT OF BRIGHTON' IN CHURCHILL SQUARE

... That fact was casually mentioned to Applegate by the Hove police, and shortly after they left a revolver shot was heard and Applegate was with a wound in the head. He died shortly afterwards in hospital... Applegate looked upon Shinn as a daughter... 'We were walking in Patcham and she suddenly said. "Oh Wally, I do feel ill." She fell forward on her face. She died on her way to hospital.' Before he was found shot Applegate had a made a statement which will probably be read at the inquest and it's possible that it will help to elucidate the mystery of Miss Shinn's death."

FRIDAY 12th OCTOBER 1984

The Grand Hotel on Brighton seafront was bombed by IRA member Patrick Magee. The plan was to assassinate Prime Minister Margaret Thatcher, and her cabinet, who were staying at the hotel for the Conservative Party conference next door at the Brighton Centre. The bomb detonated at 2:54am – Thatcher was still awake, preparing her speech for the next day – and badly damaged her bathroom. Alistair McAlpine persuaded Marks & Spencer to open early the following day so those who had lost their clothes could purchase new garments. Magee had stayed in the hotel under the false name of Roy Walsh four weeks prior to the bombing and planted the device, with a long-delay timer, in the bathroom wall in room 629. Sussex Police traced and eliminated 800 people from 50 countries who had stayed at the hotel in the month before the attack. Only Walsh could not be accounted for, but his true identity was finally revealed when a palm print on a hotel registration card matched a print taken from Magee years earlier when he was first arrested as a juvenile in Norwich, where he grew up. The incident killed five people and injured 34.

THURSDAY 13th OCTOBER 2005

The BBC reported how squabbling couples were advised to seek counselling after a war of words – using six-foot-wide banners. Adorning a 'JBS' signature, the first sign, displayed over the A27 bypass in Hollingbury, declared; 'Wendy, I want a divorce.' A couple of days later, she retorted with: 'No way. You are the cheat!' A spokesman for Sussex Police said permission had to be given for signs to be put up, commenting; "This may seem amusing but our job is casualty reduction."

TUESDAY 14th OCTOBER 1651

There were no children waving flags for the town's first royal visit! Following the defeat at Worcester, King Charles travelled to Sussex with Lord Wilmot in the hope of escaping to France. Eventually, through association, he was introduced to Nicholas Tettersell who agreed to take two passengers to France for £60 in his small coal brig, the *Surprise*. Tettersell recognised the King and demanded a fee of £200. Charles, Wilmot, Tettersell and a crew of four sailed for Fécamp and arrived the next morning. Tettersell was granted the rank of captain in the Navy and was given command of the *Monk* from 1661. In December 1663, Tettersell and his family were granted a pension of £100 per annum for 99 years. The event is remembered annually by the Royal Escape yacht race – the largest cross-Channel race outside of the Solent that starts between Brighton's piers – and by the Royal Escape public house on Marine Parade, now Audio.

WEDNESDAY 14th OCTOBER 1998

Brighton & Hove Albion fanzine *Scars and Stripes* hosted 'Fans and Bands United' at the Paradox nightclub, West Street, Brighton. England's 3-0 win over Luxembourg was shown in the adjacent Club Barcelona before The Levellers, Buster Bloodvessel and the Fish Brothers performed to over 1,000 Albion fans. The event raised over £4,000 for the football club.

THURSDAY 15th OCTOBER 1964

Dennis Hobden became the first Labour MP in Brighton, or anywhere in Sussex, when he was elected by the people of Kemp Town. Amazingly, he won his seat – with 22,308 – by just seven votes from the Conservative candidate, David James!

FRIDAY 15th OCTOBER 2004

Brighton and Hove was granted Fairtrade City status. The initiative aimed to promote Fairtrade certified goods in the area and by October 2009, over 400 British towns – and 300-plus worldwide – were awarded the status by the Fairtrade Foundation.

THURSDAY 16th OCTOBER 1958

Blue Peter was aired for the first time on the BBC. Brighton and Hove resident Biddy Baxter MBE was the show's editor from 1965 to 1988 and devised much of the format that is still broadcast today. In 2009, Baxter published a selection of children's letters received by the *Blue Peter* team, including one from a nine-year-old Anthony Hollander who wanted to become a doctor. He went on to become Professor of Rheumatology and Tissue Engineering at Bristol University, and said that he owes his career to Ms Baxter; "If her letter had shown any hint of ridicule or disbelief I might perhaps never have trained to become a ...

... medical scientist or been driven to achieve the impossible dream, and really make a difference to a human being's life."

FRIDAY 16th OCTOBER 1987

In the early hours, the worst storm in south-east England since 1703 was starting to wake the sleeping residents of Brighton and Hove from their collective slumber. Gale force winds reached speeds of over 100 miles per hour, bringing down power lines, raising roofs, battering buildings and overturning cars. Mature trees were uprooted and the peripheral trees of The Level were particularly hit. The Royal Pavilion, undergoing repairs at the time, was also seriously damaged as its protective plastic sheeting was shredded, scaffolding collapsed and, disastrously, the tip of one of the building's minarets, weighing two tonnes, crashed through the roof of the recently restored Music Room. BBC1's *Breakfast Time* programme was broadcast from a single-position emergency studio in central London, reinforcing an impression of national emergency.

WEDNESDAY 17th OCTOBER 1956

Headline in *The Times*: 'CONCRETE RAFTS AS CAR PARKS.' Chief Constable of Brighton, Charles Ridge, decided that building concrete rafts on the foreshore was a remedy for the town's traffic problems. The beach car parks would stretch for some 400 yards from West Street to the Fish Market and would accommodate 200 vehicles. A subway was suggested and cars leaving the beach would use a ramp to infiltrate into the main seafront stream of traffic.

TUESDAY 18th OCTOBER 2005

Joanne Lees took the stand at Bradley Murdoch's trial – for murdering her boyfriend Peter Falconio – in Darwin, Australia. The drug runner was accused, and eventually found guilty, of murdering Falconio on a road outside Alice Springs in July 2001. The couple had been driving around the country in a camper van and were allegedly flagged down by the 47-year-old who shot Falconio before binding Lees' hands together and putting her in his Ute. She escaped and hid in the outback. The pair had lived in Brighton while he studied at the University of Brighton. On this day, she was asked if she could identify her boyfriend's attacker. She looked at Bradley Murdoch – who has always protested his innocence – and said: "I'm looking at him." New evidence emerged in July 2011 when it was revealed that a new suspect may have been prematurely released.

MONDAY 19th OCTOBER 1891

The New Hippodrome Circus in North Road was opened to the public. It soon became the Eden Theatre, and then the Grand Theatre in 1905. The impressive venue could hold 5,000 spectators in its pomp and the building's inaugural evening produced a couple of interesting acts; Mephisto, a contortionist known as the boneless wonder, and Professor Fredrick's miniature circus of performing cats, mice, rats and monkeys. One monkey climbed a rope to the ceiling then jumped and floated down on a tiny parachute! By May 1961, the structure was a furniture factory and was gutted by a spectacular fire. *The Brighton & Hove Herald* reported: "There was a noise like gunfire as the roof crashed in. Sixty firemen from Brighton, Hove, Southwick and Lewes fought to control flames which leaped more than eighty feet into the night sky..."

SUNDAY 19th OCTOBER 1851

A truly great Brightonian, Magnus Volk was born at number 40 (then 35) Western Road, Brighton. A famous inventor, the son of a German immigrant clockmaker married Anna Banfield and lived at 40 Preston Road; they had seven children. In about 1879, Volk established the first telephone link in Brighton, to his friend William Jago's house in nearby Springfield Road, and a year later fitted his own house with electric lights. In 1883 arguably his lasting legacy, the eponymous electric railway on Brighton seafront, began construction. The modern incarnation of the line runs between terminal stations at Aquarium and Black Rock. In the same year, Volk fitted the Royal Pavilion with electric lights and 12 months later completed the illumination of The Dome, Corn Exchange, museum, art gallery, library, and Pavilion grounds. By 1887, Volk was in debt, had sold his house, and was declared bankrupt. In 1888 he built an electric car for HM Sultan Abdul Hamid of Turkey then moved his family to Clapham, running electric launches on the Thames for a living before returning to Brighton in 1892. He continued with his inventions, but made his last public appearance at the opening of his new Black Rock Station, a couple of weeks before his death on May 20th 1937. He is buried at St Wulfran's Church, Ovingdean.

SATURDAY 20th OCTOBER 1984

The day many Albion fans had been waiting for... the new roof on the North Stand! The crowd of just 10,000 didn't exactly 'raise' the new £200,000 structure during a turgid 0-0 stalemate with Barnsley. The first thousand entrants were given a free foam hand, leftovers from the FA Cup Final appearance 18 months earlier. Gary Howlett, provider of the first goal on that memorable day, made his last appearance for the ...

... club. The game was so poor that manager Chris Cattlin fined himself a week's wages!

FRIDAY 21st OCTOBER 2005

To commemorate Vice-Admiral Horatio Nelson's victory over the combined French and Spanish fleets at the Battle of Trafalgar 200 years earlier, Brighton's oldest hotel, the Old Ship, hosted a celebratory event. As John Blackman, president, HMS Suffolk Association, pointed out; "Trafalgar was not just one of those dreary battles in the pantheon of our historic victories. It had the most profound effect upon European affairs. That one battle set the seal upon Napoleon's destruction and gave the whole of Europe 100 years of peace." The Old Ship Hotel's earliest record dates from 1665 when it was owned by Richard Gilham, but may date from the previous century as an unnamed house was owned by a Richard and John Gilham in 1559. There's a fair chance it derived its name from being partly constructed from ship timbers. By 1750, the Old Ship was the property of William Hicks who, investing in Brighton's newly-found prosperity as a health resort, built a splendid new public function room by 1759. The building hosted many of the important functions in the town for years, and was used for town meetings, petty sessions, and meetings of the town commissioners in the late eighteenth and early nineteenth centuries. It was the town's post office until 1777. In 1794, the hotel gained a frontage overlooking the sea. The facade was altered in 1895, but the Old Ship Rooms remain in Ship Street at the rear of the hotel and are Grade II listed. The ballroom hosted many a grand occasion from the Prince Regent's Ball in 1819, to Nicolo Paganini's violin recital in 1831 and the Banquet celebrating the opening of the London to Brighton Railway in 1841.

SUNDAY 22nd OCTOBER 2000

A Room for Romeo Brass – a comedy drama film directed and written by Shane Meadows – was shown at the European Union Film Festival in Singapore. The film marked the acting debut of Paddy Considine, who gained a first-class degree in photography at the Faculty of Arts and Architecture at the University of Brighton. Considine co-wrote *This Is England* with Shane Meadows, who he met at Burton College in 1990.

MONDAY 23rd OCTOBER 2006

To celebrate the BT speaking clock reaching its 70th year, a competition was launched to find the new voice. Applicants were invited to leave telephone recordings of their dulcet tones, with the proceeds of each call going to Children in Need. Brighton and Hove resident Sara Mendes ...

THE PALACE PIER AT DUSK. ©BRETT MENDOZA

BRIGHTON PIER

... da Costa, a telemarketer and part-time voiceover artist, was announced as the winner on BBC One's *Children in Need* three weeks later.

SATURDAY 24th OCTOBER 1896

Sir Albert Sassoon died in Brighton, aged 78. The British Indian philanthropist and merchant was born in Baghdad, a member of a family that had resided there since the beginning of the 16th century, having been expelled from Spain in the 1490s. Albert was educated in India and became head of the family firm on his father's passing in 1864. He was a major benefactor to Bombay (now Mumbai), donating the Sassoon Dock. In 1873 he visited England and received the freedom of the city of London and became Baronet Sassoon in 1890. Shortly before his death, Albert built the Sassoon Mausoleum on St George's Road, Kemp Town at the junction with Paston Place, and his body was removed in 1933, to be reburied in the Willesden Jewish Cemetery in London, after his grandson Phillip sold the building. During World War II it served as an air-raid shelter before it was purchased by the adjacent Hanbury Arms pub in 1953 and transformed into a function room. Now an established nightclub, the venue has staged many famous – and infamous – events over the years, none more so than perennial Brighton favourites Stick It On, still going strong after making the city dance for over a decade.

WEDNESDAY 24th OCTOBER 1934

Brighton & Hove Albion, the Brighton Bears, Sussex County Cricket Club, Steve Ovett, Sally Gunnell and Chris Eubank have had spells of varying length in the Brighton and Hove sporting limelight but there was a time when another sport grabbed the local, and sometimes national, headlines. The Brighton Tigers ice hockey club played their first-ever fixture on this day, beating Richmond Hawks 4-2, at the Brighton Stadium. Crowds reached 4,000 for the Thursday night games and the roar of the Tigers fans could often be heard near the top of West Street. The original 1935 side was formed when London promoter Claude Langdon took over the newly converted ice rink and entered the Tigers in the professional English National League – which predominantly consisted of Canadians as the sport was relatively unknown in Britain at the time – alongside six teams from the London area. The Tigers, resplendent in their black and yellow kit, packed in the locals right up until the advent of World War II. After the hostilities, the club entered its golden era winning the English National League in 1946/47 and 1947/48, the English Autumn Cup 1946/47 and 1950/51, the British National League 1957/58, the British Autumn Cup 1956/57 and 1958/59 and the British Championship in 1960. Tragically, the Tigers' home, the Brighton Sports Stadium, was demolished in 1965 to make way for Churchill Square.

SUNDAY 25th OCTOBER 1964

The Beatles – in front of 4,000 screaming fans – topped the bill at The Hippodrome in Middle Street, Brighton. *The Brighton & Hove Herald* said; "...On Sunday, the experienced walls of The Hippodrome were almost shattered by the Big Scream, when thousands of teenage, and sub-teenage, girls reached the peak of Beatles worship... At first, there were more white-helmeted policemen and magpie-uniformed St John Ambulance officials than fans... the curtain rises... for the next 30 minutes bedlam is let loose... The noise is only just endurable... It's like hearing a Beatles record played over a solitary loudspeaker during a football match, acclaimed mostly by women." The venue opened in 1897 as the Brighton Ice Rink but was enlarged and converted into a circus and theatre by 1901. The Hippodrome became the town's principal variety theatre, was enlarged again in 1939, closed as a theatre in 1965 and, after a brief spell as a television film studio, became the Mecca Bingo Club in 1967. Designated a Grade II listed building in 1985, the building is vacant.

SATURDAY 26th OCTOBER 1996

Over 1,000 Albion fans marched from Brighton Station, via Western Road, Church Road and up George Street, to the Goldstone Ground in a peaceful demonstration against Bill Archer, Greg Stanley and David Bellotti. The latter was forced from his seat after a firework was thrown during the Third Division 0-0 draw with Fulham.

SUNDAY 27th OCTOBER 1974

The second episode of the original *Heidi* – adapted from the 1880 book by Swiss author Johanna Spyri about a young girl in her grandfather's care, set in the Alps – was aired on British television. Dame Flora Robson played the grandmother. The actress, born in 1902, had a distinguished career after showing recital promise from the age of just five. She made her stage debut at 19 and used her looks – 5ft 10 ins. high forehead, wide mouth and imposing nose – to good effect playing Queen Elizabeth I in both *Fire Over England* (1937) and *The Sea Hawk* (1940), and the Empress Elizabeth in Alexander Korda's *Catherine the Great* (1934). Nominated for an Academy Award for Best Supporting Actress for her role as Ingrid Bergman's servant in *Saratoga Trunk* (1945), she played royal confidante Ftatateeta, to Vivien Leigh's Queen Cleopatra, in ...

... the screen adaptation of George Bernhard Shaw's *Caesar and Cleopatra* in the same year. Created a Commander of the Order of the British Empire (CBE) in 1952, she was raised to Dame Commander (DBE) in 1960, an award which was partly for her charity work, which she carried on until her death in 1984. After 50 years on the silver screen, Dame Flora retired to Wykeham Terrace, Brighton where she resided with her two sisters, Margaret and Shela, and became President of the Brighton Little Theatre. She never married, or had children, and passed away, aged 82.

TUESDAY 28th OCTOBER 1817

The Times reported: "Forty thousand leeches, among other articles, were imported last week from France to Brighton, the whole lot packed in clean straw, in which state, it is said, they will live two months without water."

THURSDAY 28th OCTOBER 1926

'The maker of modern Brighton', Sir Herbert Carden, was made an honorary freeman of the borough. Serving on the council, he was responsible for Patcham's incorporation into the borough of Brighton – hence the two 'pylons that straddle the A23 marking the northern border – and was hugely influential in the town embracing telephone and tramway systems, and road widening. He purchased large swathes of downland – which he resold to the corporation for the same amount to defeat unfair pricing – to protect water supplies and to provide recreational facilities for the towns' inhabitants. Knighted in 1930 – he died 11 years later, aged 74 or 75 (his exact date of birth is unknown) – not all of his ideas were greeted with complete enthusiasm! He advocated the rebuilding of the entire seafront from Kemp Town to Hove, in 1930s Embassy Court style, and the demolition of the Royal Pavilion!

THURSDAY 29th OCTOBER 1959

Unbelievably, Hove Borough Council renewed their attempt to turn the beautiful Brunswick Square into a car park! A similar proposal was rejected in 1946, but only after an appeal from the magistrates' court. Today – mercifully – the idea was thrown out. The opposition was led by the Regency Society.

WEDNESDAY 30th OCTOBER 1963

Miss Southern Belle was transmitted on ITV in the Brighton and Hove area. Two months earlier saw a plea for more young ladies to enter the Miss Brighton competition. As an incentive, potential entrants were informed that first prize was '£20 cash'. Other carrots included a pair of shoes, a swimsuit of their choice, and a haircut for their appearance on television. Jackie Peterson won and went on to 'represent' the town at the Miss Southern Belle competition.

SATURDAY 31st OCTOBER 1953

The All Blacks came to Hove! A Southern Counties side, in their all white kit, entertained the world-famous New Zealand rugby outfit at the Greyhound Stadium in Nevill Road. A crowd of 10,000 was an excellent figure for a town – it was the first rugby match of any significance – not known for its odd-shaped-ball following (insert own gag here). The visitors scored 21, of their final tally of 24, points in the first half of a game that saw violent winds and a downpour.

NOVEMBER

MONDAY 1st NOVEMBER 1869

Preston Station's platforms welcomed passengers for the first time. Built primarily to serve the upper- and middle-class Clermont estate, it was rebuilt with two island platforms – and renamed Preston Park Station – when the direct line to Hove, the Cliftonville Spur, was constructed in 1879.

THURSDAY 2nd NOVEMBER 1972

Well known for playing Ronnie Mitchell in *EastEnders*, Samantha Womack (née Janus) was born in Brighton. The niece of Angie Best, a former wife of George Best, she left home at 15 for a life in London squats. The actress first came to prominence in 1991, when she represented the UK in the Eurovision Song Contest with *A Message To Your Heart*. She appeared in all 18 episodes of cult BBC2 comedy *Game On* where she played the nymphomaniac Mandy Wilkins.

MONDAY 3rd NOVEMBER 1975

A 22-year-old student decided to set fire to the Royal Pavilion! He threw a can of petrol through the Music Room window, ignited it, and setting himself on fire. In a matter of seconds the whole window area was ablaze. Fortunately, the security team were nearby and assisted the fire brigade – who took three hours to bring the flames under control. Thankfully, much of the furniture was removed just the day before. The arsonist was sentenced to six years' imprisonment. The reason for attempting to destroy one of Brighton's most-loved buildings: he was "annoyed with the Pavilion".

FRIDAY 4th NOVEMBER 2005

The BBC announced its plans to launch *Wannabes*, an interactive web-based soap opera about young people in Brighton next year. The programme, aimed at 14- to 18-year-olds, would follow the trials and tribulations of a group of youngsters attempting to start creative careers in music, television and film.

FRIDAY 5th NOVEMBER 1999

The East Brighton College of Media Arts installed closed circuit television cameras in its toilets to try to stop pupils smoking. Principal Tony Garwood said the aim was to also prevent graffiti, and to make them a 'safe' environment for younger children. Some pupils complained that their privacy was being violated.

WEDNESDAY 6th NOVEMBER 1805

Referring to the Battle of Trafalgar 16 days earlier, Mrs Fitzherbert's friend Mrs Creevey wrote; "When I got to the Pavilion last night... the Prince sat down beside me directly, and I told him my headache had me late, and he was very affectionate... Harry Gray has just come in with the news of a great victory at sea and poor Nelson being killed..." The Battle of Trafalgar public house on Guildford Street commemorates the conflict and was built in the same year.

WEDNESDAY 7th NOVEMBER 1764

Over 40 years before the Theatre Royal was conceived a barn, on the northern side of Castle Square, was used by Charles Johnson's company – for the first time today – and each year until August 1770. The seasons were necessarily short because the building was required for the harvest.

SUNDAY 8th NOVEMBER 1884

Two months after the informal opening of Preston Park, Mayor Arthur Cox officially did the job. Brighton Corporation's first – and largest – public park was purchased a year earlier as 67 acres of meadowland from the Bennett-Stanford family of Preston Manor. £22,900 was spent on landscaping with trees, flower beds, carriage drives, walks, tennis courts and bowling-greens and a chalet café – which housed the park police in the upper rooms – in the centre of the park which opened in 1887. The park was remodelled in 1928 with additional bowling greens, tennis courts and netball courts. Unveiled in May 1987, a statue of Brighton-born athlete Steve Ovett once stood near the south entrance but was frequently vandalised, and subsequently stolen. The cycle track, in the north of the park, regularly attracted post-war crowds of around 3,000 to 5,000 and was used for an England versus France international athletics meeting in 1925. Nowadays, Preston Park is home of the annual Pride festival – since 1991 – and numerous events throughout the year.

MONDAY 8th NOVEMBER 1841

Long before Snappy Snaps and Boots, Brighton's first photographic studio opened at 57 Marine Parade, a large house situated on the eastern seafront.

FRIDAY 9th NOVEMBER 1951

Broadcaster and travel writer Pete McCarthy was born in Lancashire. He attended Leicester University, where he studied literature, before aspiring to a career in comedy and co-founding 'Cliffhanger Theatre' ...

... in Brighton. In the 1980s, Pete began writing television scripts and jokes for comedians Mel Smith and Griff Rhys Jones and was also a compère for the Comedy Store in London. He made travel films before winning the Critic's Award for Best Comedy in 1990 with his piece *The Hangover Show*, which was nominated for a Perrier Award at the Edinburgh Festival Fringe. During the early to mid-1990s, Pete presented a Brighton-based TV programme *The Pier*, a 'what's on' guide of local area listings in theatre and arts. In March 1998, Pete explored Ireland over a six-month period – from the south to the north-west – resulting in *McCarthy's Bar*, which sold over a million copies. Pete intended to write a third book but tragically died of cancer at the Royal Sussex Hospital on October 6th 2004.

WEDNESDAY 10th NOVEMBER 1965

A place where the youth of Brighton and Hove discovered the joys of overpriced drinks, bad aftershave, even worse haircuts and the opposite sex, the Top Rank Suite became the catalyst for a thousand relationships, and many more hangovers. The site of the Kingswest complex was partially cleared pre-war for a proposed winter garden, but the buildings fronting King's Road, Kent Street and West Street were not demolished until 1963. The first phase of the vast West Street/Churchill Square redevelopment area, the original plans included a banqueting hall, restaurant, cinema and car park on the adjacent Sports Stadium site. In December 1966, tenpin bowling and an ice rink opened – which could be converted into a conference hall for 6,000 delegates – but only lasted four years. In the summer of 1972, a £500,000 refit converted the lower floors into several separate dance halls and bars, and the upper floor, the former ice rink, became a triple-screen Odeon cinema complex. Further changes were completed in May 1987 when an arcade from King's Road to West Street was opened, adding café-bars and shops to the facilities of the Odeon, Busby's discotheque, and the Top Rank Suite. The building's exterior is generally considered to be hideous. The 'gold' aluminium south-facing roof was intended to glitter in the sun and to give the impression of floating as a band of reflected light at night. Oh well.

WEDNESDAY 11th NOVEMBER 1992

The Argus reported that Jamaican reggae performer Buju Banton was to be dropped from the multi-cultural WOMAD festival in Brighton. The 19-year-old's *Boom Bye Bye* song contained lyrics encouraging people to kill homosexuals. Gay and lesbian activists were furious at the prospect of the Rastafarian on stage the following month at the ...

WEST STREET

Brighton is full of mystery, intrigue and fun
Even for those who read The Sun,
Off the train, don't look left, head for the treat
That awaits you; the soulless vacuum, West Street.

Grow up here, it's where you go, under age
Then you learn, what's all the rage,
The town's other jewels, depending on taste
North Laine, St James', The Lanes, make haste.

Each town has a zone
Populated by a clueless clone,
Enticed by big brands, shit beers, theme bars
Naff tats, mass produced clobber, fight scars.

Open your mind, meander off the beaten track
Have a think, 'what isn't cack?',
Explore the town, expel the obvious
Discover the real Brighton, dirty and glorious.

... Brighton Centre. Initially, WOMAD stated Banton would appear as the organisation 'did not vet artists on the basis of political, sexual or religious beliefs' but changed their stance when Banton refused to alter the track's content. Banton told WOMAD; "I do not advocate violence against anyone and it was never my intention to incite violent acts with *Boom Bye Bye*. However, I must state that I do not condone homosexuality as this lifestyle runs contrary to my religious beliefs." WOMAD dropped the Jamaican and three other acts from his label, Penthouse. A spokesman from OUTrights said loud opposition had got the decision overturned.

THURSDAY 12th NOVEMBER 2009

The BBC reported the paucity of office space in the centre of Brighton. New media companies suggested that buildings lacked air-conditioning and the capability to provide the necessary internet and power connections for technologically progressive businesses.

FRIDAY 13th NOVEMBER 1987

A block of flats collapsed without warning in Marine Parade, Kemp Town. At approximately three in the morning, the walls crumbled in seconds as a vast hole appeared directly beneath the terrace. Tons of rubble smashed into vehicles and pipes fractured, causing a potentially lethal cocktail as emergency services battled to cut off supplies. The Brighton Police tow squad, who usually charged £67 for illegally parked cars, removed vehicles in danger, for no cost. Aren't they lovely?

SATURDAY 14th NOVEMBER 1896

The Emancipation Run from London to Brighton celebrated the passing into law of the *Locomotives on the Highway Act*, which raised the speed limit for 'light locomotives' from 4 mph to 14 mph and abolished the requirement for these vehicles to be preceded by a man on foot. The law required the aforementioned man to carry a red flag but the requirement was actually abolished in 1878. However, the *Locomotive Act* was still widely known as the 'Red Flag Act' and a red flag was symbolically destroyed at the start of the Emancipation Run. Now an annual event that takes place on the first Sunday of every November, the original run consisted of over 30 pioneer motorists who set off from London on the rough roads to Sussex. Only 14 of the starters actually made the journey, and some evidence exists that one car was taken by rail and covered with mud before crossing the finishing line! The next run was staged in 1927 as a re-enactment of the 1896 event and organised by the motoring editor of the *Daily Sketch*. From 1930 to the present day the event has been owned and professionally organised by The Royal Automobile Club. Not a race but an endurance of man and machine, the London to Brighton Veteran Car Run attracts some 500 automobiles with an eligibility criteria that requires the cars to be of four- or three-wheel design and certification of construction prior to January 1st 1905. The world's longest-running motoring event is attended by enthusiasts from across the globe.

WEDNESDAY 15th NOVEMBER 1972

Jessica Hynes (née Stevenson) was born in Lewisham, London, but was educated and grew up in Brighton. She is best known for her role as Cheryl in *The Royle Family* and for writing and starring in revered TV comedy *Spaced*.

FRIDAY 16th NOVEMBER 1792

Henry Wagner, Vicar of Brighton from 1824 until 1870, was born at 93 Pall Mall, London, the son of wealthy hatter Melchior Henry Wagner, and grandson of Henry Michell, Vicar of Brighton 1744 to 1789. He married Elizabeth Douglas in 1823 and a year later accepted the benefice of Brighton and West Blatchington. Elizabeth fell ill after giving birth to their son Arthur and eventually died in 1829. At the beginning of Wagner's incumbency there were just 3,000 free sittings in the town's churches, despite something in the order of 20,000 poor people living in Brighton. Both Henry and Arthur Wagner devoted much of their lives to improving this situation, and Henry Wagner himself had six churches built; only St John's and St Paul's survive. Wagner died in 1870.

SUNDAY 17th NOVEMBER 1940

Eric Gill died aged 58. Born in Brighton, the British sculptor, typeface designer – he is responsible for the Gill Sans font – stonecutter and printmaker was a controversial figure. His well-known religious views contrasted with his paraphiliac – a biomedical term used to describe sexual arousal to objects, situations, or individuals that are not part of normative stimulation – behaviour exposed in his 1989 biography.

TUESDAY 18th NOVEMBER 2003

A Canadian who knows nothing about football was plucked off a Brighton street to play a lead role in a film about the world's most popular sport. Patrick Micallef, who worked in a mortgage call centre, was spotted by a director as he left his office. One screen test later the Seven Dials resident was cast in the independent flick *The Penalty* ...

... *King*, shot in and around Brighton. Patrick, 43, said: "I was just leaving the office when I was stopped by Chris. He said he liked the way I looked. I then did a day's shooting with Nick Bartlett, whose last film was *Gangs of New York*."

TUESDAY 19th NOVEMBER 2002

Brighton resident Bert Hobden wrote to *The Argus* enquiring as to the whereabouts of The Dome's theatre organ. The four-manual 40-rank instrument had to be removed during building and refurbishment works. Nicholas Dodds, chief executive of the famous building, replied: "The organ was built especially for the Dome concert hall in the 1930s... Restoration is a long and delicate process, with the instrument needing to be in a completely dust-free environment... We hope to unveil the full splendour of the organ in late spring 2003."

TUESDAY 20th NOVEMBER 2007

Former ITN newsreader Ed Mitchell (b. 1953) filed for bankruptcy. A few months earlier the national press had discovered the former television presenter was sleeping rough on Hove seafront. In 2008, friend and Brighton resident Carol Barnes made a documentary *Saving Ed Mitchell* that showed his struggle with huge credit card debts, alcoholism and homelessness. He subsequently abstained from drinking for three years and authored a best-selling book, *From Headlines to Hard Times*.

WEDNESDAY 21st NOVEMBER 1894

Undoubtedly one of Brighton finest sons, Max Miller was born in Hereford Street. He tried various jobs after leaving school including labouring, delivering milk, selling fish and chips, caddying at Brighton & Hove Golf Course and was also a trained motor mechanic. Volunteering for the army on the outbreak of war in 1914, he joined the Royal Sussex Regiment. On demob in 1919, he joined an alfresco theatre on Brighton beach before forming a brief double act with his wife, Kathleen – who coined the phrase 'cheeky chappie' – who then went on to mastermind his solo career. After almost a decade of nationwide revue shows, Max finally appeared at the London Palladium in 1930. Preferring solo performance, his act on a variety bill usually lasted between 20 and 30 minutes and would commence with the orchestra playing his signature tune, *Mary from the Dairy*. A spotlight aimed on the curtain by the wings would anticipate his appearance and a buzz would ripple through the audience. Master of the double entendre, Max would sometimes wait for up to ten seconds until he appeared to rapturous applause. He would walk to the microphone and just stand there in his costume, a gloriously colourful suit with plus-fours, a kipper tie and trilby and wait for the laughter, knowing he had the audience in the palm of his hand. Max – who never swore on stage and disapproved of those who did – was very much a southern English comedian and preferred being booked in theatres in London or the south, so he could return to his beloved Brighton after a show. In 1932, he embarked on his only overseas tour, when he sailed to Cape Town to appear in South Africa. Max worked as a solo act in variety for years and once earned a record-breaking £1,025 in a week at the Coventry Hippodrome in February, 1943. Lionel Hale, *Daily Mail* theatre critic, described Max as the 'gold of the music hall'. Max appeared in three Royal Variety Performances (1931, 1937 and 1950) and in the last show he was only given six minutes, while American comedian Jack Benny got 20. Livid, he abandoned his script and continued for a further six minutes, much to the chagrin of producer Val Parnell, who, in fury, told Max that he would never work for him again. He recovered and was soon back on radio and television, although his appearances on the box were never a great success. The new medium did not suit his style; the feedback only a live theatre audience could give was his oxygen. He died of a heart attack in 1963.

SUNDAY 22nd NOVEMBER 1953

Following the Brighton Tigers' game against Streatham at the Sports Stadium in West Street, Charlie Connell stepped down as supporters' club vocal director. After 18 years' loyal service, Charlie's retirement was the result of a change in employment and abode. After years of working as a cake confectioner and living in Southover Street, he took on the role of storeman at the London department store D H Evans. "Set 'em alight, set 'em alight, who's the team to set 'em alight? T-I-G-E-R-S... TIGERS!"

SATURDAY 23rd NOVEMBER 2002

Brighton hairdresser Willie Hendry was under 24-hour armed guard in Port Harcourt, Nigeria, after the Miss World contest exploded into a full-scale riot. At least 105 people were killed when trouble escalated, sparked by outrage over next month's controversial beauty pageant. Chief stylist for the annual competition, Hendry said: "We're all very worried. You never know where the violence is going to strike next."

TUESDAY 24th NOVEMBER 1998

The Royal Albion Hotel on Brighton seafront went up in flames. More than 70 firefighters and 16 fire engines tackled the blaze, which ripped through the 151-room hotel; there were no casualties and 160 ...

... guests and staff were safely accounted for. A spokesman for Brighton & Hove Council said that the fire broke out in a ground-floor kitchen and spread, via a vent, up to the sixth floor and into the bedrooms. Flames could be seen from the roof as smoke spread across the town. Guest Tom Grinyer described how he just had time to change into jeans and a T-shirt when awoken by the fire alarm at 8.20am. "The moment I opened the bedroom door, I could smell smoke and there were fire engines on the scene very quickly so I knew it was serious. The wind was blowing a gale which obviously helped to fan the flames." Many of the guests were delegates who were attending the Public and Commercial Services Union conference. At one point, fire crews were pumping seawater from the nearby beach as part of their efforts to bring the flames under control.

MONDAY 25th NOVEMBER 1901

The Brighton Corporation's electric tramway system finally commenced service after initial plans were mooted in 1864, 1879 and 1883. The first car – bedecked, as all vehicles were, in burgundy and white – was ceremonially driven by the mayor John Stafford from the initial terminus at the southern end of Victoria Gardens and along Lewes Road to Preston Barracks. Fares were a penny, for any distance, throughout the 9.5-mile system. The routes – trams ran every four to five minutes – were known by the initial letter of a road or location along it, e.g: B) Beaconsfield, E) Elm Grove, L) Lewes, Q) Queen's Park, and S) Station. Typical journey times from the Old Steine were: Brighton Station (eight minutes); Preston Barracks (15); Fiveways (18); Race Hill (18); Tivoli Crescent (20), and Rock Gardens (27).

SATURDAY 25th NOVEMBER 1934

Edith Constance Drew-Bear was found dead, fully clothed, in a concrete water tank on the edge of East Brighton golf course. She had met her partner, Percy Anderson, for a seafront stroll that afternoon and was discovered around 5pm. The police tracked him to his house in Lennox Street, Brighton, soaked to the skin, with a pistol. He appeared shocked at her death and denied all knowledge. All evidence pointed the finger at him; his scarf pulled tightly around her neck, five bullet wounds, and he was soaking, but with sea water. He was sentenced to hang at Wandsworth Prison on April 16th 1935. Some of Anderson's family had been troubled by mental health issues and he suffered from severe headaches after being struck by a golf ball aged 12. His character never in doubt, and championed by neighbours and friends alike, his defence suggested he had suffered a masked attack of epilepsy; hence the no recollection of her death, or the dip in the sea. Despite over 100,000 signatures being collected against his hanging, and a sympathetic crowd outside the gates, the executioner did his worst as the clock struck nine.

SATURDAY 26th NOVEMBER 1887

The Brighton Co-Operative Society was founded at a meeting at the Coffee Palace, 29 Duke Street. Formally established on January 1st 1888 with 200 members, the first store was opened at 32 North Road on May 16th 1888. After the Great War, numbers increased to 10,000 by 1921.

SATURDAY 27th NOVEMBER 1965

Albion thrashed Southend United 9-1 in this Third Division clash; just a fortnight after putting one more past Wisbech Town! The goals, in front of 11,124 Goldstone fans, came from Jimmy Collins, Johnny Goodchild (2), Wally Gould, Jack Smith (3) and Charlie Livesey (2).

FRIDAY 28th NOVEMBER 1896

Running 2.93 miles from the terminus of his other electric railway at the Banjo Groyne, the brainchild of Magnus Volk, the Brighton and Rottingdean Seashore Electric Railway – the 'Daddy Long Legs' – was officially opened. The twin tracks were laid to an overall gauge of 18 feet on concrete blocks built into the chalk foreshore about 60 to 100 yards from the cliffs. Just a week after opening, the railway was severely damaged by the storm that wrecked the Chain Pier. The single car was seven metres off the ground and slowed considerably at high tide. In 1900, the council decided to build a beach protection barrier, which required the line to divert around it. Without finances to do so, Volk closed the railway a year later.

WEDNESDAY 28th NOVEMBER 1956

David Van Day came into the world in Brighton. Famously a member of pop duo Dollar with Thereza Bazar in the early 1980s, he declared himself bankrupt during a legal dispute over the band name 'Bucks Fizz' with original band member Mike Nolan in 2002. Shortly after, the tabloid press renamed him 'Burger Van Day' when he was discovered flipping burgers from a van in central Brighton.

MONDAY 29th NOVEMBER 1971

Police were called to the Royal Pavilion hotel yesterday when four German members of the Northern League were attacked by ten men ...

... as they dined, reported *The Times*. "Two of them were hit by plates and had hospital treatment for cuts on the face. The attackers threw a smoke bomb in the hotel lobby and escaped in the confusion. The fighting began half an hour before the annual rally of the Northern League, which has strong views on immigration, was due to begin. Mr Jan Kruis, a Dutchman, the secretary-general, said:'We believe this was the work of some left-wing group. They were barbarians. Ten of them attacked our members from behind. The league is not a Nazi organisation or fascist, or anything like that. We are a non-political organisation concerned only with the culture and history of European peoples'."

MONDAY 30th NOVEMBER 1874

One of Great Britain's most iconic figures, Sir Winston Churchill, was born, two months prematurely, at Blenheim Palace, Oxfordshire. Before joining the famous Harrow School in April 1888, the future Prime Minister was educated at Brunswick School, 29/30 Brunswick Road, Hove. The rest, as they say, is history...

DECEMBER

SATURDAY 1st DECEMBER 1866

Colonel Sir George Everest died aged 76. Surveyor-General of India from 1830 to 1843, the Welshman was largely responsible for completing the section of the Great Trigonometric Survey of India along the meridian arc from the south of India, extending north to Nepal, a distance of approximately 1,491 miles, which commenced in 1806 and lasted several decades. In 1865, Mount Everest was named in his honour, despite his objections. He is buried at St Andrew's, in Hove.

THURSDAY 2nd DECEMBER 1965

Four months after its first UK showing, and 16 months behind the US release in August 1964, *Mary Poppins* hit the big screen in Spain. The perennial Christmas favourite featuring Julie Andrews and mockney Dick Van Dyke also starred Brighton-born actor Arthur Treacher in his last film role – the constable – aged 70.

TUESDAY 3rd DECEMBER 1996

Hated Brighton & Hove Albion chief executive David Bellotti was driven from the West Stand directors' box for the last time as fans surged across the pitch from the North Stand. It made no difference as Albion lost 3-2 at home to Darlington to go nine points adrift at the bottom of the basement division...

TUESDAY 4th DECEMBER 2007

Radio Reverb launched a light-hearted business show – giving people the chance to tell the world what really goes on in their office – called *Brighton Behind The Scenes*, presented by local events manager Anna Carey. "It is a good opportunity for businesses to break down social barriers with the public. Often more serious industries, such as law and finance, can sometimes seem unapproachable and radio provides a great way to break down any stereotypes and put a friendly voice behind the corporate image."

SATURDAY 5th DECEMBER 1835

The English language has evolved significantly over the last 180-odd years. A great example features an attempted seaside raid in today's *Brighton Gazette*: "About 5 o'clock last Saturday morning an attempt was made to run a cargo of contraband spirits opposite Hove, but it proved ineffectual. One of the coastguard, whilst on duty near the spot, observed on a hillock at a short distance several men, upon which he involuntarily ejaculated, 'I am done,' almost at the same moment he was seized by several persons, but being an athletic man, he contrived in the scuffle to draw a pistol from his belt and fire it, which brought some of his comrades to his assistance, and the smugglers fled up the country. The crew... leaving behind... 76 tubs of spirits, which were crept up by the coastguard, and landed at the southern extremity of the Chain Pier..."

THURSDAY 5th DECEMBER 1957

The Brighton Tigers' most famous game was played at the Brighton Stadium. The Red Army squad had stunned the world only 18 months earlier by winning the ice hockey gold medal at their first Winter Olympics, in Cortina d'Ampezzo, Italy. The Big Red Machine, as they were christened, had already brushed aside a couple of other National League sides – on full-size rinks – on their tour. The West Street arena's surface was only 175 by 75 feet – and known as the Goaltenders' Graveyard. Captained by Red Kurz, the Tigers gave themselves a mountain to climb, going behind 3-0. As the Soviets took their collective feet off the gas, Brighton fought back and, incredibly, scored six goals without reply! BBC commentator Alan Weeks, Tigers' press officer, was speechless. "I've got nothing to say," he told the press afterwards. "I'd only blubber. I'm excited, exhausted and stunned." The commentator credited the club with giving him his 'big break' with the Beeb in the early 1950s. He steadfastly fought for a building to replace the Sports Stadium up until his death in 1996, aged 72.

SUNDAY 5th DECEMBER 1999

The former *Argus* building in North Road was devastated by a huge fire. People were evacuated as flames tore through the building at 6am, streets were cordoned off and ten fire engines were sent to the scene. Gas cylinders inside the disused building exploded to send glass and debris flying and two firefighters were injured; one was hurled across the road by the explosion, and a second was taken to the Royal Sussex Hospital with a leg injury after debris landed on him. Station officer Douglas Moody said: "I came in from Hove and I could see smoke over the whole of central Brighton." More than 30 residents were evacuated and police broke down the doors of houses where they received no reply to ensure nobody was left in the danger zone.

FRIDAY 6th DECEMBER 1867

The West Street Concert Hall swung opens its doors for the first time. Home to musical concerts and lectures, in 1877 the building was converted into a roller-skating rink and five years later was virtually destroyed by a gas explosion and fire which left only the frontage ...

... standing. The roller-skating hall was reconstructed in 1892. In 1911 the building was converted into a 2,000-seat cinema – the Grand Picture Palace which was renamed the Coliseum in 1918 – but following another serious fire it reopened as the famous Sherry's Dance Hall. Together with the Regent, Sherry's dominated Brighton's pre-war nightlife but in 1949 it was converted back into a roller-skating rink and then became the Ritz amusement arcade in the 1960s. The intricate Italianate facade of the 1892 building was demolished in 1969 when it was remodelled as a nightclub and amusement arcade. Its many incarnations include the Pink Coconut, Tru, The Paradox, and Creation.

TUESDAY 7th DECEMBER 2004

Six special needs students were admitted to the Royal Sussex County Hospital after drinking a corrosive substance thought to be dishwasher liquid. They were among seven who drank the fluid – which was mixed with orange cordial – while visiting Plumpton College near Lewes on Tuesday. The youngsters suffered burning to their mouths and throats, as well as abdominal pain.

SUNDAY 8th DECEMBER 1985

Despite Withdean Stadium being home to Brighton & Hove Albion for 12 years, the venue's highest crowd was in fact for an American Football game! To be fair, though, the capacity was only 9,000 during the association football club's tenure. Brighton B52s hosted City College of San Francisco – where former American Footballer and now imprisoned O J Simpson graduated in 1966 – in front of 12,000 fans. The North Americans were far too strong for their hosts and ran out convincing 72-0 winners.

SATURDAY 9th DECEMBER 1967

For the second day running, and two months before its official launch, Radio Brighton broadcast to the people of Brighton and Hove as an emergency blizzard service. Only the fifth local station in the country, the station initially covered the coastal area from Shoreham to Peacehaven with 75 watts on 88.1 MHz from Whitehawk Hill. In October 1983, Radio Brighton became BBC Radio Sussex.

SATURDAY 10th DECEMBER 1910

A Visit to the Seaside (1908) was released in the United States. Directed by George Albert Smith of Hove – who patented a camera and projector system and owned St Anne's Well Pleasure Gardens – the film is ...

VIEW FROM THE HEAD OF THE WEST PIER BACK TOWARDS BRIGHTON SEAFRONT, INCLUDING THE SPIRED METROPOLE HOTEL ON THE RIGHT

... recognised as historically important and was the first successful one in natural colour, filmed using Kinemacolor. The eight-minute short shows people doing 'activities' in Brighton.

WEDNESDAY 11th DECEMBER 1935

Lord Derby opened an information bureau at Victoria Station in London. Paid for by the Brighton Corporation, the booth – manned by multi-lingual staff – was to provide details of the town's attractions and accommodation.

TUESDAY 11th DECEMBER 1979

The ill-fated *Athina B* – built as the *Kojima Maru* at Hiroshima in 1968, renamed *Hung Wei* in 1973 and *Nina Pa* in 1976, before being sold and renamed in 1979, sailing under the Greek flag – set sail from the Azores laden with 3,000 tonnes of pumice. Her destination was Shoreham, a few miles west of the Palace Pier. During the voyage, she had problems with her generator, gyro compass and radar, and docked at La Rochelle, northern France, for repairs. On arrival at Shoreham on January 20th, force 7 or 8 winds meant she was unable to enter the harbour – hindered by a loss of power from the engines – and a Mayday call was issued. The Shoreham Lifeboat took off half the crew and the captain's family, with the rest being rescued the following morning after four attempts. The ship drifted eastwards, running aground to the east of the Palace Pier with a broken back. A restaurant bears its name, a painting hangs in Brighton Museum, and the ship anchor is on display on the seafront.

WEDNESDAY 12th DECEMBER 1821

The extraordinary Phoebe Hessell passed away after a truly amazing life. Born Phoebe Smith in 1713, she was best known for disguising herself as a man to serve in the British Army, probably to be with her lover, Samuel Golding. She enlisted in the 5th Regiment of Foot to serve alongside him, and saw duty in the West Indies and Gibraltar. Both were wounded in the Battle of Fontenoy in 1745 and she finally revealed her position; they were both discharged and married. They had nine children – eight died in infancy – and the survivor died at sea. After Golding died, she moved to Brighton to marry fisherman Thomas Hessell, who died when she was 80, and supported herself by selling fish in and around the town. Her evidence was instrumental in securing the conviction and execution of highwayman James Rooke and she was granted a pension of half a guinea a week by the Prince Regent in 1808. As the oldest inhabitant in the town she was entitled to sit beside the vicar at a Napoleonic celebration dinner on The Level in August 1814 and she attended the Prince Regent's coronation parade in Brighton in 1820. She died, aged 108.

TUESDAY 13th DECEMBER 2005

After the city council had rejected a park and ride scheme at Patcham Court Farm, the plans for a 'rapid transport system' that would connect the marina, Royal Sussex County Hospital, the King Alfred development, Brighton station and the Brighton Centre, were revised.

MONDAY 14th DECEMBER 1829

Unfortunately, Brighton has long been referred to as 'London by the sea' (not in my house). On this day, *The Times* featured a story on Brighton Statistics: "The town of Brighton is drawn up facing the sea, like a regiment of soldiers; the picked company of tall fellows on the flanks, the best men front... the shabby little slouching dogs at the rear. Or, as we all know Brighton is an offset of London, imagine the town-houses to have set off racing down to the shore of Sussex... the Albion Hotel... standing foremost of all, with its toes in the water... just so is Brighton ranged, staring with all its best at the water. In the rear, all is secondary and shabby... The grenadier company is Brunswick-terrace, occupying the right flank; while the left is Kemp-town, a skeleton detachment lost in the clouds..." [All sic].

SATURDAY 15th DECEMBER 1990

WBO middleweight champion Chris Eubank paraded his champion's belt before the Goldstone Ground crowd in Hove, prior to the game with Barnsley, to promote his forthcoming fight with Dan Sherry at the Brighton Centre.

TUESDAY 16th DECEMBER 2008

The cast-iron frame of Brighton's 130-year-old bandstand was returned to its rightful place on the promenade near the bottom of Preston Street following renovation work. The 1884 Grade II listed landmark, which had been derelict for 30 years, was restored in Derbyshire and was known as the 'birdcage' because of its dome roof and latticed arches.

TUESDAY 17th DECEMBER 1974

The M23 motorway opened bypassing Crawley and Redhill. Upgrades between Patcham and Warninglid crossroads began construction in 1990.

FRIDAY 18th DECEMBER 1818

William Moon was born in Kent. By 1839, he was totally blind and living with his widowed mother and sister Mary in Brighton. He taught ...

... the embossed reading codes devised by Frere, Lucas, Alston and Gall to local blind boys, who found them difficult to learn, and devised a newer system, Moon Type – based on simplified letters – which he designed to be easier to grasp. For almost 50 years, The Moon Printing Works operated from 104-106 Queen's Road producing books and magazines in Moon's tactile typography, designed to be read by touch.

SUNDAY 19th DECEMBER 1971

Swimmer Karen Pickering MBE was born in Brighton. She made her international debut in 1986 and went on to win 73 titles on the national and international stage; four-times world champion, 14 European Championship medals, 38 British Championship titles and 13 Commonwealth Games medals (four gold). Karen now runs swim schools and is an in-demand after-dinner speaker.

MONDAY 20th DECEMBER 1948

Sir Charles Aubrey Smith died from pneumonia in Beverly Hills, Los Angeles, aged 85. His body was cremated and nine months later, in accordance with his wishes, his ashes were interred in his mother's grave at St Leonard's churchyard in Hove. He played cricket for Sussex intermittently between 1882 and 1892 and was renowned for his oddly curved bowling run-up that earned him the nickname 'Round the Corner Smith'. He prospected for gold in South Africa in the late 1890s and then treaded the boards in London before pursuing the bright lights of Hollywood where he became known as a professional Englishman. His bushy eyebrows, beady eyes, handlebar moustache and height of 6ft 4ins. made him one of the most recognisable faces of the time and he appeared in dozens of films including *Cleopatra* (1934), *The Prisoner of Zenda* (1937), *Dr Jekyll and Mr Hyde* (1941) and *Little Women*, his last, in 1948. In 1932, as the Bodyline series raged in Australia, he founded the Hollywood Cricket Club – that would boast David Niven, Laurence Olivier, Leslie Howard and Boris Karloff as members – and supervised the building of a field and pavilion. Los Angeles City Council bulldozed the area and converted it into an equestrian centre for the 1984 Olympics. A blue plaque commemorates his stay at 19 Albany Villas, Hove.

WEDNESDAY 21st DECEMBER 2005

Originally planned for one minute past midnight – the government updated a piece of legislation in order to fit in with new time constraints for heterosexual marriage, which stipulated that a ceremony can only be conducted between the hours of 8am and 6pm – the Reverend Debbie Gaston and her partner of 16 years, Elaine Cook, became the first same-sex couple to register under the Civil Partnership Bill. Debbie said; "Elaine and I have waited many years to be able to make this kind of commitment to each other and we both see the Civil Partnership Bill as a huge step in the right direction for equality. God is so central to our lives and our relationship that we couldn't do the whole day without mentioning God and having him in it somewhere." Elaine concluded; "It says to the world this is what I want to do, this is who I am, and this is who I'm in love with."

WEDNESDAY 22nd DECEMBER 1943

John Joseph Dorgan was hanged for his wife's murder at Wandsworth Prison by Thomas Pierrepoint. The story began in July of the same year. Dorgan had started to sell items to random people on the streets, and in the pubs, of central Brighton. The 47-year-old, who had served his country with distinction during World War I, lived with his 60-year-old spouse, Florence, and a lodger Charlie, in Madeira Place. The selling continued apace. Florence's daughter, Beatrice, from a previous marriage, had called round to the flat and been unable to locate her mother. Beatrice eventually spotted her step-father through a basement window heavily involved in discussion with two men. Dorgan asked if she had seen Florence and then informed her that she had actually left to walk to her daughter's house in Hollingdean Terrace. A neighbour informed Beatrice that Dorgan had been selling her mother's possessions and she grew more suspicious. By 7.00am the following morning he was entering the Norfolk Arms – it was open early to cater for the neighbouring market traders – and flashing the cash. His next three ports of call resulted in 'drinks all round' again. Meanwhile, Charlie had finished his shift at the Old Ship and returned home to change. Bending down to place his boots under his bed, he noticed a bundle of out-of-place clothes, went to pull them out and realised, to his horror, that is was the body of his landlady Florence. Dorgan was soon apprehended in a taxi and confessed all immediately. The couple had argued and he had become frustrated by her nagging.

MONDAY 23rd DECEMBER 1782

Thomas Kemp, one of Brighton's most influential residents, came into the world just up the road in Lewes. Graduating from Cambridge in 1805, he married Frances Baring – they had six daughters and four sons – and became Member of Parliament for Lewes when he won his father's former seat in 1811. Twelve years later, after resigning, and forming a religious cult, Kemp conjured up a grandiose plan for a fashionable estate east of Brighton that was to bear his name and, hopefully, boost his bank balance. Initially unsuccessful, he fell deeper into debt selling ...

... various plots around the town and then purchasing the Wick estate in Hove. He was renowned for his philanthropic land gifts for worthy causes, such as hospital and gaols.

THURSDAY 24th DECEMBER 1903

The towns' first motor-bus ran from Hove Town Hall to Castle Square. The United Company still ran four horse routes until December 8th 1916 when the last horse-bus ran from Carlisle Road, Hove, to Brighton Station.

WEDNESDAY 25th DECEMBER 1940

With World War II raging football continued under the auspices of the War South League and the team – all five of them; one senior player, three juniors and (as a guest) Bolton's Jimmy Ithell – travelled to Carrow Road, Norwich. After borrowing some juniors from the home side and servicemen from the crowd, Albion let the Canaries flap to a rather unflattering 18 goals without reply!

FRIDAY 25th DECEMBER 1992

Brighton's Grand Hotel featured in the Christmas edition of *Only Fools & Horses...* Del inherited Grandad's old allotment and received a summons from the council, ordering him to remove a public health hazard – the barrels contain an unknown yellow substance – from his land. Trigger and Denzil help remove the offending chemicals and end up dumping them 'in a pond'. When Del sees the high price of produce in an organic shop he develops an interest in gardening and invites the owner, Myles, to the allotment to advise him on growing vegetables. A mysterious water source is spotted – which Del calls the Peckham Spring – and Myles suggests that if the water is pure, it could be bottled and sold. Rodney notices that the 'spring water' is actually coming from a nearby tap connected to a hose and concealed by rocks. Uncle Albert secures an authenticity certificate by using real mineral water and the Trotters set up a production line by filling up bottles from his kitchen tap. Peckham Spring Water quickly becomes one of Myles' biggest-selling products and sales are further boosted by the drought warnings issued by the local water board, who believe there is a serious underground leak due to the high volume of water being used by Del. The Trotters earn enough money for a Christmas holiday at the Grand Hotel and in the final scene – as Del, Rodney and Uncle Albert go to sleep – the news reports that a local reservoir had been contaminated by a yellow liquid. As a blissfully unaware Del switches off the light, a bottle of Peckham Spring glows on his bedside table!

SATURDAY 26th DECEMBER 2009

Brighton & Hove City Council got into the festive spirit by sending out their army of jobsworths – sorry, traffic wardens – to patrol the streets of the city. The previous month Brighton and Hove was named and shamed as the country's parking fine capital, with more collected in the city than in any other local authority outside London.

SATURDAY 27th DECEMBER 1856

Depending on the source, the Hove Amber Cup was discovered in 1851, 1852, 1854, 1856 or 1858. With this in mind, I've picked today's date as the probable time. It is likely to be incorrect but it is safe to say that the cup – made from northern Europe amber, thus suggesting early trade links between England and the Baltic – is over 3,500 years old. Considered to be one of Britain's most important Bronze Age finds, it was unearthed during the excavation of a burial mound in readiness for the construction of Palmeira Avenue in Hove. Among the finds in an oak coffin carved from a single tree trunk were bone fragments, a dagger, a whetstone and an axe head.

FRIDAY 28th DECEMBER 1956

Renowned violinist Nigel Kennedy came into the world in Brighton. From a family of musicians, he has many family members in Australia and only met his father aged 11. He joined the Liverpool Philharmonic Orchestra aged 24 and now lives in Poland.

SUNDAY 29th DECEMBER 2002

A section of the West Pier fell into the sea. The temporary walkway connecting the concert hall and the pavilion completely collapsed at approximately 9.20am. Geoff Lockwood, chief executive of the West Pier Trust, said: "What we don't know is what will happen now – it is a grand old structure and it has survived for a long time so it might be OK."

THURSDAY 30th DECEMBER 2004

The BBC website reported on Seagulls Ska entering the charts. The Albion fans released a version of The Piranhas' classic *Tom Hark* to raise awareness on the fight for Falmer Stadium. The song eventually reached 17 in the Top 40.

SUNDAY 31st DECEMBER 1826

Tom Sayers was baptised in Brighton. The talented boxer, just 5ft 8ins and 11 stone, was born in the North Laine slum of Pimlico – a filth-ridden area densely populated with fishermen and their families – six months ...

... earlier. His fighting career lasted from 1849 until 1860, when a match billed as the contest for the 'World Championship' with American John C Heenan in Farnborough ended in disarray. Sayers seemed to have the advantage when after 37 rounds and two hours and 20 minutes of fighting, the crowd broke into the ring and the fight was declared a draw. Such was his popularity that a public subscription was made for his benefit which raised £3,000, given to him on condition he retired from the ring. He bought a house in London and soon the illiterate Tom succumbed to the temptations that idleness and money can provide, including an ill-advised investment in a touring circus. Just five years after his retirement, he died of diabetes and tuberculosis at the age of 39. Such was his fame that his burial at Highgate Cemetery was attended by 10,000 mourners. In 1954, Sayers was elected to the Boxing Hall of Fame.

TUESDAY 31st DECEMBER 1974

Three days after his 63rd birthday, Brighton Tigers legend Bobby Lee died. Under the guidance of the Canadian – who quickly became a fan favourite, scoring 32 goals in 40 games – the Tigers won a grand slam of domestic ice hockey honours. When he returned after World War II he took on the triple role of player, coach and manager as the club entered a golden era. They won the league in the first two post-war seasons and collected three major trophies in 1946/47; league, National Tournament and Autumn Cup. The gifted stickhandler retired in 1954, aged 42, after becoming the first player to score 400 goals in the league, coming close to 500. He also played for Baltimore Orioles, Earls Court Rangers, Montreal Royals, Quebec Aces, Montreal Canadiens and Wembley Lions.

FRIDAY 31st DECEMBER 1999

Along with the rest of the world, Brighton and Hove partied like it was 1999. More than 50,000 revellers descended on the Old Steine to mark the dawn of a new millennium. Music, street theatre and fireworks entertained the vast throng. Police leave was cancelled for the night, but there was barely a sniff of trouble as revellers let their hair down for the once-in-a-lifetime event. Only nine people were arrested at the Old Steine for minor public order offences and drunkenness and Royal Sussex County Hospital only treated 12 people, mostly for drink-related injuries. Brighton inshore lifeboat became the first in the country to be called out – just three seconds after midnight – following reports of a distress flare off the marina. It was a false alarm.

BIBLIOGRAPHY

Thanks to John Denyer and Trevor Chepstow for the information on
Charlie Connell.

A History of Brighton & Hove
Ken Fines, Phillimore & Co. Ltd (2002)

Brighton Between the Wars
James S. Gray, Cinderhill Books (1975)

Brighton & Hove Albion On This Day
Dan Tester, Pitch Publishing (2007)

Brighton & Hove Albion Miscellany
Paul Camillin, Pavilion (2006)

Brighton: The Sixties
Christopher Horlock, S. B. Publications (2006)

East Sussex Events
David Arscott, Phillimore & Co. Ltd (2003)

Gay News No. 31
6-19th September 1973

Life in Brighton
Clifford Musgrave, John Hallewell Publications (1981)

In The News Brighton
David Arscott, Sutton Publishing (2002)

Murderous Sussex. The executed of the Twentieth Century
John J. Eddleston, The Breedon Books Publishing Company (1997)

The New Encyclopaedia of Brighton
Rose Collis, Brighton & Hove Libraries (2010)

The Encyclopaedia of Brighton
Timothy Carder (1990)

bbc.co.uk
argus.co.uk
songwritershalloffame.org
ukwhoswho.com
brightontsunami.com/
greatbritainhockey.co.uk
rpbridge.net/1a00.htm
brightonourstory.co.uk
britishpathe.com
dailymail.co.uk
library.kent.ac.uk
maxmiller.org
fopa.co.uk/history.aspx
brightoncarnival.co.uk
tiff.shutterchance.com
suite101.com
sallygunnell.com
independent.co.uk
spartacus.schoolnet.co.uk/
   RAbrighton.htm
brightonbears.com/
infotrac.galegroup.com
roedean.co.uk
sussexcricket.co.uk
mybrightonandhove.org.uk
visitbrighton.com
azhockey.com
profootballresearchers.org
chattri.com
mybrightonandhove.org.uk
shorehamairport.co.uk/
stpetersbrighton.org/
brighton-racecourse.co.uk
theguardian.co.uk
arthurlloyd.co.uk
southernwater.co.uk
pathenews.co.uk
sussexyachtclub.org.uk
visitbrighton.com

brighton-hove-rpml.org.uk/
   Libraries
brighton.ilb.org.uk/news
imdb.com/title/tt0079766/
terramedia.co.uk
brightontigers.com
independent.co.uk/sport
nationalarchives.gov.uk
st-dunstans.org.uk
reese.org
junk-tv.com/trunk.htm
screenonline.org.uk/film/
   id/486826/index.html
movie-locations.com/movies/q/
   quadrophenia.html
ambassadortickets.com
en.wikipedia.org/wiki/List_of_
   people_from_Brighton_and_
   Hove
spartacus.schoolnet.co.uk
thebodyshop.com
en.academic.ru/dic.nsf/
   enwiki/2228929
cricinfo.com
westpier.co.uk/
modrevival.net/Quadrophenia.
   html
number10.gov.uk
gutenberg.net.au
athletics-weekly.com
fathom.com
terramedia.co.uk
tony-hawks.com
mixmag.net
cemeteryscribes.com/showmap.
   php?cemeteryID=69
sports-reference.com/olympics
scip.org.uk/moon/theman.htm
plato.stanford.edu/entries/ryle/